CANADIANS AND THE NATURAL ENVIRONMENT TO THE TWENTY-FIRST CENTURY

D0082643

Canadians' relationship with the natural world has been informed by two major impulses: the need to exploit natural resources and the desire to protect them. In *Canadians and the Natural Environment to the Twenty-First Century*, Neil Forkey explores these two opposing impulses and fills in the middle ground to reveal a complex and evolving narrative of the interplay between humans and the natural world in Canada. He provides the historical foundation necessary to understand contemporary environmental issues in Canada.

Forkey's engaging survey addresses significant events and perspectives from across the country over the past four hundred years: the early conception of Canada as a storehouse of natural resources and a site for scientific exploration; resource exploitation and conservation in the nineteenth and twentieth centuries and their socio-economic implications; Romanticism and the preservation of nature in the Victorian era; the era of environmentalism that began after World War II; and Aboriginal points of view. *Canadians and the Natural Environment to the Twenty-First Century* provides an accessible synthesis of Canadian environmental history that takes into account the important temporal, demographic, social, economic, political, and cultural forces that affect the natural environment.

(Themes in Canadian History)

NEIL S. FORKEY is a visiting assistant professor in the Department of Canadian Studies at St. Lawrence University.

THEMES IN CANADIAN HISTORY

Editors: Craig Heron and Colin Coates

NEIL S. FORKEY

Canadians and the Natural Environment to the Twenty-First Century

PROPERTY OF
SENECA COLLEGE
LIBRARIES
NEWNHAM CAMPUS

WITHDRAWN FEB 1 2 2013

UNIVERSITY OF TORONTO PRESS
Toronto Buffalo London

© University of Toronto Press 2012
Toronto Buffalo London
www.utppublishing.com
Printed in Canada

ISBN 978-0-8020-9022-5 (cloth)
ISBN 978-0-8020-4896-7 (paper)

Printed on acid-free, 100% post-consumer recycled paper with
vegetable-based inks

Library and Archives Canada Cataloguing in Publication
Forkey, Neil S., 1964–
Canadians and the natural environment to the twenty-first
century / Neil S. Forkey.

(Themes in Canadian history)
Includes bibliographical references and index.
ISBN 978-0-8020-9022-5 (bound)   ISBN 978-0-8020-4896-7 (pbk.)

1. Human ecology – Canada – History.   2. Natural resources –
Canada – History.   3. Nature – Effect of human beings on –
Canada – History.   4. Environmental policy – Canada –
History.   5. Canada – Environmental conditions – History.
I. Title.   II. Series: Themes in Canadian history

GF511.F67 2012   304.20971   C2012-901583-0

University of Toronto Press acknowledges the financial assistance
to its publishing program of the Canada Council for the Arts and
the Ontario Arts Council.

 Canada Council   Conseil des Arts
for the Arts   du Canada   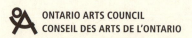 ONTARIO ARTS COUNCIL
                                 CONSEIL DES ARTS DE L'ONTARIO

University of Toronto Press acknowledges the financial support of
the Government of Canada through the Canada Book Fund for
its publishing activities.

To my family. For Roseline, this project began in Paris, summer 2004, what a wonderful memory. This is for you for more reasons than I can ever count. Pierre-Laurent, I hope you will always be fascinated by the tall trees of Parc Laurier. And, Éléonore, don't ever stop gazing and wondering at the stars.

To my father, John F. Forkey, from whom I learned so much.

Contents

Acknowledgments

Several people have been instrumental in seeing this project come to fruition. At the University of Toronto Press, Len Husband saw my proposal as promising and accepted it as part of the Themes in Canadian History Series. Colin Coates was an extraordinary editor: encouraging, enthusiastic, and patient at every turn. He challenged me to think about new ways of organizing material and offered sound advice, especially in his area of expertise, New France and Quebec. I also appreciated the perceptive comments of the external reviewer commissioned by the press. An early version of the manuscript benefitted from comments received at a meeting of the environmental history study group Quelques Arpents de Neige (associated with the Network in Canadian History and Environment, NiCHE). My Canadian Studies colleagues at St Lawrence University, Joseph T. Jockel and Robert W. Thacker, provided institutional support as well as a stimulating intellectual setting that would help any professor to continue to grow. Dr Mary Graham and Dr Rick Welsh were always there to help in more ways than one. My family deserves the greatest thanks. My wife, Dr Roseline Tremblay, has waited patiently to see this manuscript in print. Our children Pierre-Laurent and Éléonore are now able to finally see what Papa has for so long been typing on his laptop. You three, more than any others, should share in whatever good comes from this project. Of course, I alone am responsible for any errors or omissions.

CANADIANS AND THE NATURAL ENVIRONMENT
TO THE TWENTY-FIRST CENTURY

Introduction

What does it mean to read Canadian history through its environment? Examining the natural landscape or created cityscape as a historical source makes visible the human impression, or imprint. We notice the actions and ideas that shaped, refashioned, or made sense of a given place. We also gain insight into what past peoples valued, what they preferred as living space, and what they accessed as sources of sustenance.

At the surface level, Canadians' experience with the natural world has been informed by two major impulses. The first is the need to exploit natural resources, while the second is the desire to protect them. Admittedly, this is a rather blunt way to begin the text, but it will prove useful. If we take these two opposing impulses as our starting point, we can effectively fill in the middle ground with more subtle and nuanced investigations to reveal a complex story. Temporal, demographic, social, economic, political, and cultural forces have coalesced to create the contemporary microenvironments that make up Canada. The cast of characters that orchestrated these changes is vast: hunters, fishers, farmers, woods workers, miners, naturalists, foresters, businesspeople, bureaucrats, household consumers, novelists, university students, automobile drivers, and so on. Canadians from all regions and walks of life have been actors in tandem with the natural world. The story told here involves us all, since we each have some interaction with our natural surroundings.

Environmental history places humans and nature together in the same historical space. Although it might be tempting to think of human and environmental histories as two separate and exclusive domains, such compartmentalization hardly reflects the reality. It is impossible to fathom these two narratives as discrete given the influence of nature, resources, wilderness symbolism, and the like on people in Canadian history. There is a strong case to be made for the idea that humans and nature are mutually entwined in one related narrative of Canada's past. The objective of this book is to make that case.

This modest-sized text covers over four hundred years of Canadian history. Necessity dictates that there be a compression of data and a distillation of material. The emphasis here is on clearly presenting the main ideas, illustrated by strong examples, in the most efficient and economical manner. The first chapter examines initial encounters with the place that became Canada, up to the early twentieth century. This entry into the subject matter provides an overview of the early conception of Canada as a storehouse of aquatic, forest, and agricultural staples, as well as a site for natural history study and scientific exploration. The second chapter takes up both the exploitation and conservation of resources. In so doing, the various socio-economic realities of such attempts are explored. Romanticism and the preservation of nature are the focus of chapter three. Chapter four probes the more recent history following the Second World War. This so-called era of environmentalism is an unfinished story. In so many instances, we search for ways to accord the natural world some sort of sustainable future, while simultaneously pursuing fossil fuel use that contributes to climate change. Aboriginal points of view are found in nearly every chapter, but receive specific consideration in chapter five. While a comprehensive analysis of current environmental debates is beyond the scope of this work, readers will find a narrative that places the natural world squarely in the broader Canadian story.

1

The Classification of Canada's Environments (1600s to Early 1900s)

Since Aboriginal and European peoples' first encounters with this land, natural resources have been essential to Canada's unfolding story. Fish, furs, timber, agricultural produce, minerals, and hydroelectric bounty continued to propel Canada's economy until at least the middle of the twentieth century. Between the seventeenth and twentieth centuries, Canada first became consolidated as a French possession, later came into the hands of the British, and finally became an independent nation whose own federal and provincial governments encouraged the exploitation of the environment for economic gains. Throughout this period, Western science probed the utility of staples extraction in the northern half of the North American continent. The classification and naming of geological, meteorological, and biological aspects of this new land was paramount to the economic endeavours at hand, and this scientific inquiry is an essential starting point here. Concurrent with the exploitative impulse, natural historians of the past also discovered the finer details of these unfamiliar ecosystems and gave inspiration to those who later worked to celebrate and protect the living world.

First Encounters with the Land

Natural resources are what initially attracted humans to the place that became known as Canada. The Aboriginal peoples, after all, were migrants; they came from Siberia across an ice bridge that once spanned the Bering Strait. They searched for large mammals and were either unable to return to their place of origin, or found sustenance in the environment they encountered. They became, in Alfred W. Crosby's phrase, the 'geographic avant-garde'; that is, they learned to master their natural surroundings and turn challenges to their advantage (18).

Much later, Europeans arrived as part of the 'technological avant-garde' (ibid.). From the Middle East north to Europe, they were more urban based, had domesticated animals, and had developed a mathematical understanding of the world that was expressed in a scientific curiosity. Their economic drive fed their desire for exploration. Their mapping of the solar system and advancement in sailing vessels enabled them to reach the New World. The course of human history led Europeans and Aboriginal peoples to encounter one another in a sustained manner around the sixteenth century.

Consider the path followed by the earliest inhabitants, whether Aboriginal or European. To them, Canada must have seemed a place of limitless bounty. Aboriginals hunted game of all sorts – they rushed bison off cliffs, burned forests to better hunt deer, and speared and seined fish. Where possible, they practiced horticulture, and sometimes agriculture. Trade networks flourished as well; Huron cornmeal, for example, was exchanged for Ojibwa fur pelts. Shelters and weapons were crafted from animal hides and bones as well as wood and rocks. Medicinal remedies were also found in nature, as many as five hundred of which are still in use today. Early French missionaries were impressed by the local knowledge of the Aboriginals when it came to questions of health and longevity. The Recollect missionary Chrestien Le Clercq declared the inhabitants of the Gaspé to be

nature physicians, apothecaries, and doctors, by virtue of the knowledge and experience they have of certain herbs, which they use successfully to cure ills that seem to us incurable . . . [they] generally enjoy perfect health right up to a fine old age, for they are not subject to several of the maladies which afflict us in France . . . (Le Clercq 296)

Aboriginals adapted various ecosystems to fit their needs; they manipulated the natural world in order to subsist and constructed complex trading nexuses. European newcomers, in turn, altered the land to fit their own ways of living. The land was colonized unevenly from east to west, at different times and with varying degrees of impact. Examining the first two centuries of European or Euro-Canadian entry into each region, however, often yields a similar story; environmental change was sporadic and localized.

Such was the case in New France. The lack of an overwhelming French presence before the Royal Charter of New France in 1663 (in 1608 there were only twenty-eight settlers in the colony, but by the time of the Conquest of 1760, when parts of New France were handed over to Britain, there were approximately seventy thousand) meant that these colonies still retained a pre-contact environment in many locations. As the number of French settlers increased, however, familiar European species were transplanted to North America; a phenomenon that Crosby refers to as the transfer of 'portmanteau biota' (89). Migrants from France brought European plants (e.g., wheat, rye, barley, oats, millet, buckwheat, peas, flax, hemp, cabbages, asparagus, and watermelons) and animals (horses, cows, pigs, chickens, and rats) to the new land, sinking European roots deeper into Canadian soils. It is estimated that by 1672 all the plants and animals of importance to life in the old country were present in the colony. The seigneurial system of property division, another Old World imprint (reminiscent of feudalism), parcelled out rectangular plots of land along the banks of the St Lawrence River to landlords chosen by France's king. Once the land was bounded, some forests were quickly denuded; by the 1720s a few riverine communities lamented that the forest was gone, to the detriment of users who now needed to find wood much further back from the water.

A small French population inhabited Acadia. In 1650, there were three hundred Acadians, but their numbers had risen to between fourteen thousand and eighteen thousand on the eve of their expulsion in 1755, during the Seven Years' War. Diking the marshlands is an obvious example of the ecological change they brought. In order to grow wheat while still inhabiting the aquatically rich coastline, Acadians took to creating dikes. They reclaimed land from the sea by constructing log embankments that kept the twice-daily tides from coming inland. Drainage ditches contained wooden sluices (*aboiteaux*), which were fitted with clapper valves and allowed water to drain from farmland back to the ocean, but then shut tight to prevent sea water from passing inland. An observer in 1708, N. Dièreville, was thoroughly impressed:

The ebb and flow of the Sea cannot be easily stopped, but the Acadians succeed in doing so . . . [a]n undertaking of this nature, which can only be carried on at certain Seasons when the Tides do not rise so high, costs a great deal, [and] takes many days, but the abundant crop that is harvested in the second year, after the soil has been washed by Rain water compensates for all the expense. (Clark 161)

This European-introduced technology allowed Acadian farmers, already short on labour, to put down a crop but avoid wholescale forest clearing. Similar techniques were used along the lower St Lawrence River (at Kamouraska) into the twentieth century.

By comparison, the lands west of the Ottawa River were virtual wilderness until the beginning of the nineteenth century. United Empire Loyalists sided with Britain during the American Revolution. When the English lost the war, upwards of forty thousand Loyalist migrants made British North America their new home: Nova Scotia received approximately thirty thousand, what is today Quebec took in another two thousand, and seventy-five hundred went to what would come to be called Upper Canada (and later Ontario). Hundreds more 'late loyalists' arrived during the 1790s, but sparse populations and dense forests continued to make for slow progress when it came to environmental change. By the mid-nineteenth century, after subsequent bursts of migration from the British Isles, this situation changed; within a generation Upper Canadians had become veritable 'ecological revolutionaries,' reshaping the land with their numbers and the new species of crops they introduced (Wood xvii). Wheat, corn, oats, potatoes, and hay became principal crops, while holdings of livestock evinced a farmer's rising income. Potash became the first cash crop as forests were thinned; it was created by burning wood, then constantly pouring boiling water over the ashes which turned them into liquid lye. Lye was an alkali used to make soap, glass, and bleach, among other things. Sawmills dotted riverbanks – there were over fifteen hundred by 1848, triple the amount found only eight years earlier. In the 1840s timber exploitation served as the second major pillar of the economy, resulting in the loss of one-third of the mature woodland south of the Canadian Shield. (During the next thirty years, nearly three-quarters would disappear, and on the eve of World War I, 90 per cent would be gone.)

As late as 1763, what would become the interior portion of the continent (the Prairies) was considered *terra incognita*. This large expanse was known as Rupert's Land and was possessed by the Hudson's Bay Company (HBC). The fur trade linked this region both by sea to London and overland to Montreal, where the North West Company (NWC) also competed for western furs. Following Confederation in 1867, Rupert's Land was transferred to the Dominion of Canada; the HBC received $1.5 million and continued to operate, though in a more circumscribed way. Ontarians took their ideas of husbandry and agricultural improvement with them as they moved onto the Prairies after 1870. In Manitoba, for example, legislators took a cue from their

earlier Ontario counterparts and passed laws that made
it incumbent upon farmers to remove weeds that would
endanger the vitality of the wheat crop.

The Pacific Coast's development was similar to that of the
Prairies. The fur trade predominated into the nineteenth
century and thus discouraged settlement. Captain James
Cook's 1778 contact with the Nootkas of Vancouver Island
ushered in the first wave of exchange in furs. A vibrant
maritime trade with China ensued between the 1780s and
1840s. Overland fur traders based in the south and east of
Canada also converged upon the Pacific Coast in the nineteenth century, culminating in fierce competition between
the HBC and the NWC and the ensuing merger of the
two firms in 1821 (under the HBC banner). By 1881, the
province of British Columbia counted just over fifty-three
thousand inhabitants; although nearly thirty thousand were
Aboriginal, more than nineteen thousand traced their roots
to Europe.

Up to the mid-nineteenth century only a partial resettlement by Europeans and Euro-Canadians had occurred
across Canada. Wholescale transformations were not at
hand, except in the oldest, most populated places: the St
Lawrence Valley–Lower Great Lakes axis and Acadia. Even
New Brunswick, which supplied vast quantities of pine and
spruce to the British navy for shipbuilding and other uses,
appeared to natural historian A.L. Adams in 1873 as pos-
sessing 'all the features of the primitive forests of other
portions of this continent' (Wynn, *Timber Colony* 150).
Much more pronounced physical and demographic change
became apparent after the mid-nineteenth century.

Physical Changes: Pathogens, Wildlife, Plants, and Fish

Alterations to the various ecosystems did of course happen.
The introduction of deadly pathogens from Europe to early
Canada created the most profound and tragic environmen-
tal consequences. This has been referred to as one facet

of the Columbian Exchange, whereby plants, animals, and diseases were elements of the interplay between Europe and newly discovered lands. Europeans had gradually developed immunity to many diseases such as influenza, pneumonia, whooping cough, smallpox, and typhus; Aboriginals had no such defence. The continuous contact from European urban centres afforded by French and later English ships of the HBC seems to be the most likely source of infectious diseases, as settlers, fur traders, and animals were transported in unsanitary conditions during lengthy voyages. Once Aboriginals made contact with anyone from these ships, they might in turn travel back to their own peoples where transmission continued.

Sustained French contact with Northeastern Woodlands peoples began in the early 1600s. The trade in beaver pelts was the impetus for these relations. However, the 1635 death of Samuel de Champlain, leader of the colony of New France, placed control of the colony in the hands of religious orders such as the Jesuits. The Catholic Church wished for a more religiously grounded colony in North America. Consequently, Jesuit missionaries (known as 'black robes') became more plentiful in New France during the 1630s and beyond; moreover, they lived among the Aboriginals whom they hoped to convert to Christianity. The fur traders and Jesuits' sustained presence unwittingly aided the spread of pathogens – the Montagnais, the Algonquin, and the Huron all took deathly ill with smallpox between 1634 and 1635 in the first full epidemic to strike the Northeast. In 1639, a smallpox pandemic again devastated the Algonquin; they died 'in such numbers . . . that the dogs [ate] the corpses that [could not] be buried' (Delâge 87). The subsequent season was no better: '[o]f a thousand persons baptized since the last [year], there are not twenty baptized ones out of danger of death . . . more than 260 children under seven years [have died]' (ibid.). Such 'crowd diseases' festered in places where Aboriginals lived in longhouses, as the Huron people did (their territory, the Georgian Bay region, was known as Huronia). As one section of the community became infected, the contagion easily spread to other members. In short order, disease, internal conflict among the Aboriginals themselves, and continued raids by the Iroquois Confederacy brought about Huronia's collapse by 1649. It is estimated that the Huron (and nearby Petun) population of about thirty thousand in 1634 plummeted to only twelve thousand five years later. As a direct result of the death toll among Aboriginals, the French became numerically superior in the St Lawrence Valley. In 1650, the twenty-five hundred French settlers out-numbered the two thousand Aboriginal peoples. The void left by the Huron necessitated French-managed northern posts in the interior; in the past, it was the Huron who acted as conduits between the French and northern trappers such as the Ojibwa. As the fur trade spread west, deadly smallpox epidemics struck the *petit-nord* (between the upper Great Lakes and Red River Valley) in the late 1660s, late 1730s, and again in the late 1770s. Likewise, a smallpox epidemic between 1781 and 1782 killed thousands of Aboriginals from the plains (including the Shoshone, Blackfoot, and *Gros Ventres*) to the Pacific Coast Salish.

The depletion of beaver from some sectors of New France signalled another environmental change. The Rec-ollect missionary Gabriel Sagard, after visiting the Huron in the 1620s, lamented, 'I cannot think but that the end is in sight [for the beaver]' (Krech 176). He also chronicled the actions of the Iroquois Confederacy; each year trapping parties of hundreds of men exploited confederacy lands and later those of their neighbours, thus further thinning beaver stock. By 1635, beaver were becoming scarce around Trois-Rivières. Similarly, the Jesuit historian Pierre-François de Charlevoix noted the fierce exploitation that followed the advent of the French-Aboriginal fur trade. By the early eighteenth century, he recounted, one hundred years after the fur trade commenced, less and less beaver were to be found in New France. As beaver were trapped out in one location, Aboriginals and Europeans would gradually push north and west in order to procure new pelts. By the dawn of the nineteenth century, the NWC reported erratic returns of beaver: 1,904 pounds of fur in 1801, 2,868 pounds in 1804, and 908 pounds in 1808 along the Lower Red River. The use of more efficient steel traps rather than traditional means of capture was primarily to blame for the instability in returns. Yet, competition among trappers only increased and the returns for the next half century or so demonstrate the result. Between 1803/4 and 1857, for example, the HBC estimated that in the southern portion of its territory and the northern United States, the decrease in traded furs was around one-half to two-thirds. The explorer David Thompson noted a similar lack of control concerning the overexploitation of the beaver on the West Coast in the early nineteenth century, expressing that '[e]very intelligent Man saw the poverty that would follow the destruction of the Beaver, but there were no Chiefs to control it; all was perfect liberty and equality' (Dickason, *A Concise History of Canada's First Nations* 46). In the Rocky Mountains, the situation was complicated by trespassing and poaching of beaver by so-called 'mountain men' of European extraction or by Iroquois working independently or in the employ of fur trade companies. Steel traps baited with castoreum, a concoction made from the glands of the beaver, proved especially destructive. In all these cases, market pressures can be blamed for such irrational behaviour.

On the Northwest Coast, the China fur trade prompted a case of species collapse. Sea otters were abundant in the 1780s and 1790s, as they had only been caught and skinned for local use by Aboriginals. Around this time, however, sea otter skins became attractive on the Canton market; by the 1810s they were three times more valuable than beaver fur. English, American, and Russian traders easily filled their ships with product. In 1787 on the Queen Charlotte Islands, one captain got three hundred skins in thirty minutes; two years later another captain took two hundred skins in only a few minutes time. However, the high prices spurred an aggressive hunting of the sea otter, a mammal with a low fertility rate. Female sea otters produce only one offspring per year (as compared to two to five for female sables and beaver); worse still, female fur was in greater demand, as it was of higher quality than that of the male. After 1812, paltry returns were reported by a wide variety of merchants and captains, and this continued for the next two decades. In one remarkable example, five American vessels could only procure eight hundred sea otter skins during the entire 1827 season. By the middle of the nineteenth century, the Northwest Coast had been depopulated of sea otters; in the late twentieth century, the species had to be reintroduced.

Other signs of overexploitation were visible in the ginseng trade. Long regarded in China as a remedy for countless physical ailments and general mental well-being, North American-grown ginseng root found a ready market half the world away from its source. Though ephemeral (the boom period lasted only from 1749 to 1752), the exportation of New France ginseng root to La Rochelle, France, and then to Canton created the first commercial link between Canada and China. Once the roots were harvested they needed to dry for one year; premature shipment of uncured roots lessened their quality (and price). High demand for ginseng (it fetched over 12,000 francs in 1747 and more than 400,000 by 1752 on the Canton market) spurred overharvesting and convinced cultivators to ship 'green' (poorly dried) ginseng. When the market became flooded with inferior product, the price fell, and the Canadian-harvested crop earned a poor reputation from which it never recovered. Moreover, overharvesting of the root caused its depletion to the point that it could no longer be found around the habitual settings of Montreal, causing the Aboriginal harvesters to seek out supplies in the New York colony. In a vain search for ginseng, Aboriginals even took to setting the forests of New France ablaze during the summer of 1752.

Although cod fishing (which began in the 1530s) was one of the first extractive activities to connect Europe to early Canada, it took over four hundred years for its full effect to be noticed. Basque whalers were present in and adjacent to the Gulf of St Lawrence beginning in the early sixteenth century, but their link to Canada was not nearly as strong (nor as long) as those forged through the cod fishery. French, Spanish, Portuguese, English, and New England fleets plied the waters off Newfoundland, particularly the Grand Banks. Settlement of Newfoundland was prohibited by English law in the hope of minimizing competition for cod. Many fishermen disregarded this policy, however, and remained on the island after the fishing season closed. The result was that by 1800 about twenty thousand people lived there. By the 1830s, the longest-settled areas of Newfoundland began to demonstrate cyclical declines in salt cod exports. Conception, Trinity, and Bonavista bays had grown in population and their inhabitants took to the sea to earn their living. Too many fishers were chasing fewer and fewer cod. Some longstanding merchant houses recognized what was happening and tried unsuccessfully to limit fishers' access and stem the use of more intensive technologies such as cod jiggers, trawl lines, and cod seines. (More obvious signs of overfishing emerged by the 1960s and reached the critical state by the 1990s.)

Disease and resource exploitation changed early Canada's environments. Apart from the obvious human toll, changes occurred at the local level, and were not always so obvious as to signal a drastic, wholescale transformation of the land or waters. Following soon after the traders, however, were others who desired to know more about this unfamiliar place than the quickest way to turn a profit trapping furs. Within the context of European penetration into North America, natural science served a dual purpose: to assess the material wealth of this new land and to build an understanding of how the myriad pieces fit together to create a unified whole, a web of life. In this regard, early Canadian history shares something important with that of the United States during the same period of growth and maturation. Historian Richard W. Judd cogently argues that in the American colonies to at least the 1840s, nature study informed the thinking of the giants of American environmentalism: Henry David Thoreau, John Burroughs, John Muir, and Gifford Pinchot. The core era of scientific inquiry, c. 1740 to 1840, consisted of

a practical concern for protecting those species of birds, animals, and trees deemed useful to human society; a romantic appreciation for the beauty of natural form and primitive landscape; and a close understanding of the complex biological interdependencies that sustain all natural systems. (Judd 9)

While it would be unwise to force a similar characterization upon the Canadian scene, there are some aspects of this description that ring true when assessing the activities and outlook of French and English natural historians who tried to make sense of the northern half of North America. These researchers were cataloguing and classifying resources so as to expand the wealth and knowledge of empire and nation, observing climate so as to assist agriculture, probing the life cycles and habits of flora and fauna useful to new settlers, drawing practical lessons from past treatments of the land, celebrating the sublime and picturesque qualities of nature, and finding moral teachings from natural cycles.

Natural Science Develops

To those French following the path of Jacques Cartier, Samuel de Champlain, and other explorers and traders, the land and its flora and fauna must have equally appeared as a mysterious treasure trove. Natural historians – whether they were amateurs with an interest in botany or professional scientists – gave Western civilization some of the first narratives of the land, its resources, and its potential for development. Jesuit priests provided some of the first glimpses into the natural world; their accounts are contained in the annual *Relations* they sent back to France. The priests often regarded this new land as forbidden and perplexing, more of an uncultivated garden than a place of grace and beauty. Take, for example, the mixture of wonder and trepidation evinced by Father Jérôme Lalemant's account of a meteor in late 1662, when 'fierce serpents flying through the air' lit the Quebec sky. It 'illuminated the night almost with the splendor of day, though our pleasure in beholding it was mingled with fear because of the sparks which shot out in all directions' (Greer 125). French botanizers (amateur botanists) routinely sent specimens back across the Atlantic to established collections such as the *Jardin du Roi* (the future *Muséum national d'Histoire naturelle*) in Paris. Such institutional benefactors owed a great deal to the curiosity and effort of early visitors to the colony, such as Michel Sarrazin, a military surgeon who arrived in New France in 1685. At first, he had no apparent interest in botany. However, after a brief return to France and visits to the *Jardin*, he became aware of the great task that lay before men of science, to learn about the French possessions. This epiphany owes much to his contact with members of the *Académie royale des sciences* in Paris, which was founded in 1666 and dedicated to promoting the study of natural history, especially beyond Europe. Sarrazin returned to the colony in 1697 as a correspondent of the *Académie*, a common practice among men with royal postings. He played a dual role as surgeon and botanizer and performed dissections of native animals such as the beaver, muskrat, and porcupine, and sent reports of his findings back to France for publication.

This initial sorting of species took on greater precision and meaning during the Age of Reason, or Enlightenment, as Europeans began to standardize classification systems. Among the plethora of qualities attached to this period, the quest for scientific knowledge was foremost. The precursor to this methodical approach was Sir Francis Bacon's method of inductive reasoning, which sought through empirical testing to produce practical knowledge that could benefit humankind. By the close of the Enlightenment era, the search for causality in natural phenomena had become important to the outlook of many who sought to understand the place of humans in the natural world. Especially prominent was the legacy of Carl Linnaeus, who developed a method of classification by plant family. This method advanced the idea that by determining the species of organisms, their origins could be unlocked and they could be placed into more complex categories, or genera. The system was grounded in the belief that earth's species were created by a divine presence and served specific functions in the grander scheme of life. In this sense, natural history study was purposeful in revealing a divine order. This would not be the first attempt to use scientific knowledge to reveal perceived truths.

Pehr Kalm studied in Finland under two Linnaean botanists, and later under Linnaeus himself. When Linnaeus organized a collecting trip to North America in 1747, Kalm was chosen to undertake the voyage. Kalm's instructions from the Royal Swedish Academy of Sciences were to learn as much about Canada as possible. The wisdom he received was that the Canadian climate best resembled that of Scandinavia. After spending ten months in the American colonies and consulting with the leading naturalists there, Kalm made his way to New France in late June of 1749 and stayed until late October. Throughout his sojourn he recorded information about the social life of the colonies and various details regarding flora and fauna.

Kalm was welcomed to New France by Jean-François Gaultier, a doctor and corresponding member of the *Académie royale des sciences*. Gaultier had spent five years in the colony and had cultivated interests in several branches of science. For example, he is credited with establishing Canada's first meteorological station in Quebec in 1742, from which he noted the annual migrations of birds, physical features such as the ice break-up on the St Lawrence

River, and the harvests of local farmers. As a physician, he touted the therapeutic benefits of the sulphuric water found at Baie-Saint-Paul and Les Éboulements, he was known to use indigenous plants such as spruce beer as a remedy for scurvy, and he encouraged wintergreen tea as a dietary supplement. Mineralogy also interested him, and he wrote on the geological formations he found in the colony. It was the Frenchman's skill as a botanist, however, that most aided Kalm. Gaultier was diligent in collecting and naming the various plant species he found in New France, keeping the Aboriginal names wherever possible. He was particularly original in his study of pine trees, asserting that there were four distinct types at a time when only one was thought to exist in Eastern Canada. He annually sent seeds to his counterparts for use in the *Jardin du Roi*. Accompanied by Gaultier, Kalm collected seed specimens of maple trees and maize (corn) that seemed to be hardy in the cold climate. Kalm brought these back to Europe, thus further broadening the portrait of economic possibilities to be found in Canada. Figures such as Sarrazin and Gaultier embodied the spirit of exploration and collection in a way that made the contributions of amateur French naturalists important to the larger effort of empire building.

These natural history endeavours continued at least throughout the nineteenth century in British North America. André Michaux, for example, botanized from Tadoussac to Rupert River (near James Bay) in 1792, where he observed the flora and collected seed specimens, which he sent the following year from Montreal to France. David Douglas conducted botanical excursions in Upper Canada and the Pacific Coast. From his base at Fort Vancouver (in present-day Washington State), he botanized the region. His travels took him to Rupert's Land during 1827 where he botanized extensively for the Horticultural Society of London. Perhaps the most well-known reference to his work in the Pacific Northwest is the magisterial Douglas fir. In the North, HBC traders and former military engineers carried out scientific surveys that not only bolstered company knowledge of the terrain, but also filled the needs of those in England who were curious as to the wealth of the land.

Toward an Early Ecological Understanding

Another inspiration for natural history study was the English curate Gilbert White. His 1789 book, *The Natural History of Selborne*, spurred many people across England and its possessions to seek out a holistic link with the natural world, one that made connections between the actions of species and their consequences for others, often with a reverence for divine creation. Selborne, a town in East Hampshire, England, became the Arcadia of Greek mythology (a vision of pastoralism and harmony with nature) reborn.

In Nova Scotia, Titus Smith Jr explored the colony's little-known interior at the start of the nineteenth century, later authoring a report on the resources found there. This was followed by an article in 1835 in which he hinted at the wedding of human and natural history since the era of Acadian possession of the territory. His earlier forays provided him with data that fed a hypothesis.

Smith identified two main vegetative zones, the first consisting of deciduous hardwood trees and the second made up of succulent shrubs. In both zones, soil and vegetation shaped each other. In the hardwood forest, for example, trees, branches, and leaves fell to the ground and decomposed, a cycle that was repeated year after year. The trees' roots then fed upon the built-up nutrients in the decomposed material that lay on the surface. In barren soils, the vegetable matter that lay on the ground was strongly resistant to decay, so trees and shrubs grew slowly. Moss would grow on the ground as the forests thickened. Natural fires easily seized this dry environment and left an exposed surface upon which various long-dormant seeds could germinate (e.g., raspberries, blueberries, French willow, and elderberry). This phase would last only a few years, however,

before species such as alder, fir, white birch, and poplar sup-
planted the berries. The process thus continued in a cycle,
which, when it was concluded, Smith argued 'resume[d]
nearly its former appearance . . .' (Wynn, '"On Heroes,
Hero-Worship, and the Heroic" in Environmental History'
137). Fire was an agent of change in this process. After a
burn, the charred remnants took to the air and landed on
nearby water grasses, water lilies, and other plants that grew
in lakes and ponds. Year after year, storm after storm, frag-
ments of these plants would dry and be taken by the wind,
thus helping to create yet another type of environment: the
mossy, quaking bogs that were common in the interior of
the colony.

Smith contended that the human settlement of Nova
Scotia had produced serious consequences – while '. . .
Indians carefully avoided setting the woods on fire,' Loyalist
refugees (from the American Revolution) in the eighteenth
century did just the opposite (ibid. 138). The newcomers
purposefully set the forests ablaze in order to make clear-
ings for farms and villages. They pastured cattle, which fed
upon the regenerated grasses that sprang up after the burn.
This process of anthropogenic burning was repeated to
foster more and better grazing spaces and thus encourage
larger herds. These actions weakened the remaining forests
by loosening the roots of trees and causing them to fall pre-
maturely in wind storms. Consequently, this left more fuel
on the forest floor, which then caught fire in the dry season
and hastened the deterioration of the environment. Smith
set the human-induced change of Nova Scotia in larger, global terms. Referring to the eastern Mediterranean, Smith
wrote that 'man has, by mismanagement, impoverished
some of the finest countries on earth' and argued that similar processes had occurred within the recent past in Nova
Scotia (ibid. 139). While Smith's brand of natural study
yielded both practical and cautionary conclusions, other
commentators were more literary and emotional in their
expressions.

Catharine Parr Traill wished to be remembered as the 'Canadian Gilbert White.' Her first Canada-inspired text, *The Backwoods of Canada* (1836), began as letters sent to her mother in England. In these, she recounted the entry of Anglo-Celtic settlements in the Trent watershed of Upper Canada, an area of the colony where she lived until her death at age ninety-seven. Although optimistic about the march of progress into the forests of the backcountry, she at times lamented the pace of destruction at hand. The Mississauga had burned the Rice Lake area to such an extent that forest had given way to plains, and the newcomers were felling the remaining stands. She criticized the violence with which pioneers went about denuding the country: '[m]an appears to contend with the trees of the forest as though they were his most obnoxious enemies . . . he wages war against the forest with fire and steel' (162).

In a similar vein, Philip Henry Gosse's effort to recast Quebec's Eastern Townships in Arcadian terms is noteworthy. English by birth, Gosse first reached Canada by way of Newfoundland, where he collected insects and had an interest in meteorology. He purchased land in the Eastern Townships in 1835, and hoped to become a self-styled gentleman-farmer. Though this dream never materialized, he made an even more important contribution through his book *The Canadian Naturalist* (1840). The text takes the form of a dialogue between a father and his son; Gosse used these characters as mediums through which the local flora and fauna were described. Additionally, he commented on attitudes toward nature; he believed that humans were meant to be stewards and create harmony. Gosse decried what he saw as the pointless, wasteful killing of deer. And although he hunted wolves because they attacked local farmers' sheep, Gosse nonetheless found it ridiculous to adversely view the predator:

it is absurd to say that any animal is 'fierce without provocation, and cruel without necessity' [. . .] Their thirst for blood is an irresistible instinct implanted in them by an allwise God, and the

tiger or the wolf could no more exist without slaughter, than the
sheep without cropping the herbage. (Little 66)

Gosse became one of the best-known nature writers of the
nineteenth century.

In short, the study of natural history was often used as
a means of exploring the continent and amassing a vast
inventory of knowledge on natural resources, but it could
also serve as an outlet of appreciation for the natural world,
or what was left of it in the face of intrusion by new settlers
in Canada.

Scientific Knowledge in Support of the State

As scientific study became more specialized, the ground-
work laid by this first wave of naturalists, both amateur and
professional, whetted the appetites of a new generation.
The emerging Canadian state had a vested interest in using
science to encourage resource extraction. This would lead
to increased public revenues, as the stage for economic
activity (especially in lumbering and mining) was often
Crown lands (i.e., places with no private titles). Individual
provinces and eventually the Canadian state leased timber
berths and mineral rights to private investors; revenues
raised could then be used for a multitude of public projects
such as infrastructure creation. As H.V. Nelles succinctly
explained,

Crown ownership of natural wealth was a joint legacy of the
French and British imperial traditions. In both the French
seigneurial and British freehold land systems the distinction
between possession of surface rights and ownership of the minerals underground was transmitted to the North American continent. (2–3)

Though landlords and farmers could hold titles to the
surface level, what lay beneath belonged to the Crown.
This latter fact extended to Canada's forests, as well, where

(in both the French and English cases) tall, sturdy timber was converted into naval vessels that protected imperial possessions.

Crown forests provided Canada with an abundant source of revenue and a prime place within the British Empire up to and following Confederation. The exploitation of Canada's forests started in the Maritimes, particularly in New Brunswick. Following the European quest for cod, other aquatic species, and furs, New Brunswick's forests provided the next link in the long series of Canadian staples that were joined to the European mercantile economy. At the start of the nineteenth century, the colony held a sparse population, primarily settled along rivers such as the Miramichi and Restigouche, and eventually along the St John and St Croix. Settlers often turned to work in the woods to supplement their livelihoods. When the Napoleonic Wars complicated trade within Europe, New Brunswick became Great Britain's principal bastion for timber; this continued to the 1850s. Saint John merchants capitalized on the export of timber from that port. Foodstuffs were imported by the same route. At its peak, around 1824–5, the colony exported over 240,000 tons of timber, recording similar levels up to the middle of the century. The forests were denuded, and magisterial pines, so sought after by builders of naval vessels and other ships, became hard to come by. Central Canadian forests were exploited during the eighteenth and nineteenth centuries, thus duplicating the existing pattern of lumber exportation. Quebec forests supplied product first to France, then later to Britain. The 1854 Reciprocity Treaty made it possible for Chicago and other burgeoning American midwestern centres to access Ontario pine without paying duties.

The prospect of mineral wealth excited the imaginations of public and private men in the pre-Confederation era, and this gave rise to a growing curiosity for what riches were contained in Canada's bedrock. The greatest expression of this quest for information was the Geological Survey of Canada

(GSC), which hinted at the desire for a national (or at least British North American) inventory of what lay below the earth's surface. In 1842, William Edmond Logan embarked upon this important scientific endeavour. Logan was in his early thirties when English geologist Charles Lyell posited a theory about the earth's age. Known as 'uniformitarianism,' Lyell's research indicated that the planet was a mass that was prone to internal and external alteration, especially by dynamic upheavals such as earthquakes. In other words, the planet was in an ongoing state of change. Here we see another example of science practitioners attempting to augment the body of knowledge of a popular theory. As in the case of Kalm and Linnaean botany, Logan was influenced by new ideas in geology, which in fact had even greater repercussions in other fields such as biology.

Capitalists from early Ontario and Quebec were keen on a government-sponsored survey of the United Province of Canada (as it was referred to between 1841 and 1867). They sought a systematic inventory of the potential mineral wealth. In the pre-Confederation era, there was also a push to locate and extract coal in the Canadas. Coal lay below the surface of Nova Scotia, but imperial duties acted as obstacles to intercolonial trade, and thus, for the moment, the resources of this maritime province were closed to Central Canadian capitalists. Indeed, the attraction of Nova Scotia's coal was one of the factors that drove the British North American colonies toward Confederation in 1867. In the process, more science-minded men desired evidence about what had created such geologic phenomena as the Laurentian Shield and the Rocky Mountains. In this case, science exploration went hand in hand with the search for extractable staples, or, at the very least, arable land. In fact, it could be argued that science supported the opening of the Northwest.

The Northwest presented an especially interesting case study for natural historians. Was the Canadian Northwest a mere northern extension of the 'Great American Desert' that lay south of the 49th parallel? That was the principal question in the minds of many during the first half of the nineteenth century as arable land in Upper Canada became less and less available. The 1850s witnessed a flurry of interest in determining the agricultural potential of the Northwest. Beginning in 1857, two expeditions were launched, one led by John Palliser, and the other a joint venture involving Henry Youle Hind (a chemistry professor at Trinity College in Toronto) and Simon J. Dawson (a civil engineer). Palliser first cast his eyes upon the region during an 1847–8 hunting trip. He traded on this experience and convinced the Royal Geographical Society and the British government to finance his 1857–60 scientific forays, in which he and his party explored the land from the Red River settlement to the Pacific Coast, and from the North Saskatchewan River to the 49th parallel. His report included valuable data on astronomy, meteorology, magnetisms, and geography. At nearly the same time Hind and Dawson began their venture, which was sponsored by the Canadian government. Their investigation centred only upon the area from Red River to the parklands and southern plains of what are today Manitoba and Saskatchewan.

Both parties reached similar conclusions about the region. First, they found that there were two zones, both with varying economic agricultural potential: the 'fertile belt' (a western trajectory from Red River to the Rocky Mountain foothills) and the 'arid plains,' with a dry climate, sandy soils, and abundant grass cover. This second area became known as Palliser's Triangle. Perhaps wary of the Sioux that frequented the area, neither party ventured south of the arid plains to explore an area *within* the triangle. As a result, both groups dismissed the patch along the international boundary and lying west of Wood Mountain to the Cypress Hills as a northern extension of the Great American Desert. It was not until further exploration of this zone by John Macoun in the 1870s and 1880s that its true potential to support settlement was realized. Yet the early pronouncements of Palliser, Hind, and Dawson ushered in a reassessment of the Northwest. It was no longer a worthless place, but potentially the salvation of the landless offspring of Upper Canadian farm families.

Using justification based on science, western boosters cast the region as the 'Last Best West.' The surveys reinvented the Northwest in eastern minds, particularly those of the Clear Grits and Reform parties (the future Liberal Party), whose constituencies often included agriculturalists eager to secure new lands for themselves and their children. In 1855, George Brown's newspaper, the *Globe*, reported that the last 'wild' lands in Canada's West had been sold on the western peninsula that borders the Detroit River. This message was dire to Canadian farmers. The fear of a closing frontier, or, more appropriately, the lack of arable land, was at hand. Eminent men such as George Brown, William McDougall, George Monro Grant, Charles Mair, and Sir Sandford Fleming favoured western expansion.

In 1880, John Macoun, a botanist who had previously spent time in the Northwest, returned to take another look at the so-called arid plains of Palliser's Triangle. Macoun was no opponent of progress; he saw this place as a potential home to countless settlers. And, to reinforce this belief, he traversed the area of Wood Mountain west to the Cyprus Hills, to which previous expeditions had perhaps been forced to pay scant attention. While he concurred with many of Palliser's other findings, Macoun disagreed that this stretch of land was incapable of supporting an agricultural population. He drew upon contemporary thinking on climate and argued in his report that contrary to prior assessments, it mattered little that the area received limited annual rainfall. What counted, he insisted, was the amount of precipitation during the spring and summer growing seasons. If there was enough precipitation during the crucial vegetative portion of the year, even on such a semi-arid plain, then farmers could conceivably transplant themselves to the far western fringe of the Northwest. To some, this might have seemed a gamble, but to those promoting immigration, including the federal government, Macoun's report was welcome news and aided the Canadian Pacific Railway (CPR) in laying the route west. That Macoun was appointed to the GSC in 1881 only added credence to his findings.

Interpreting Darwin

Scientific debate rarely occurs in a vacuum. In Western civilization during the modern period, no scientific debate ignited such a furore as Charles Darwin's suggestion of natural selection, first publicly pronounced in his 1859 treatise *On the Origin of Species*. Darwin drew inspiration from Lyell's suggestion that the earth was an ever-changing, living mass. Moreover, his work marked a departure from the established role of science study that Linnaeus's adherents had emphasized. No longer was it acceptable to merely add more and more knowledge to defined categories of species. The emphasis had now shifted from the static to the ever-changing.

Darwin's voyages aboard the HMS *Beagle* in the mid-1830s, which included a trip to the now-celebrated Galapagos Islands, inspired his thinking that species adapt to their surroundings in order to survive. Reliance upon the idea that divine providence gifted all species, of the world and somehow provided for them in perpetuity was (soon to be) gone. But if nature was a constantly changing and sometimes violent place where species struggled to dominate food sources, then what role did belief in a Christian God play in understanding the human presence on earth?

Darwin's ideas had a great impact upon scientists in Canada, although not without controversy. The example of John William Dawson provides insight into the complex reception the new theory received. Dawson was an unflagging advocate of professional science and the promotion of enlightened knowledge in the Dominion. Born in Pictou,

Nova Scotia, in 1820, and educated at the University of Edinburgh, Dawson became a chief promoter of McGill University when he accepted a principalship there in 1855. Science became a prime vehicle in his quest to elevate the international status of the university. He had previously cultivated contacts with Lyell and Logan. Dawson contributed to the geological mission that Logan had embarked upon, and in 1855 he published a geological investigation of Nova Scotia. Dawson also played a leading role in the creation of the Royal Society of Canada in 1883, believing that, like Great Britain and the United States, the Dominion needed a national scientific organization.

Dawson preferred the idea of constancy over time as opposed to Darwin's theory of variation and change. The problem, as Dawson saw it, lay in Darwin's methodology, wherein artificial and natural conditions were confounded. Indeed, in a twenty-page review of *On the Origins of Species* for the journal *Canadian Naturalist*, Dawson berated Darwin for leading science away from its Baconian roots of inductive reasoning and instead ushering in a mode of thinking where

instead of studying the facts in order to arrive at general principles, we shall return to the mediaeval plan of setting up dogmas based on authority only, or on metaphysical considerations of the most flimsy character, and forcibly twisting nature into conformity with their requirements. (Sheets-Pyenson 131)

In other words, Dawson claimed that Darwin had proposed a theory that challenged the prevailing scientific method by manipulating his evidence to suit a predetermined outcome. Much of Dawson's critique rested upon his entrenched religious views, which he defended until his death in 1899. Most of the scientific world, however, had accepted Darwin's theory. The beginnings of life suggested by Darwin caused those of the modern age to re-evaluate not only natural history, but the origins of humanity and its relationship to the natural environment.

Other voices joined the chorus against the theory of natural selection. The respected priest-entomologist León Provancher derided the new wave of evolutionists in print and public lecturers, and praised the divine power that he believed was responsible for the course of life on earth. Catharine Parr Traill's message that there existed an over-arching divine plan in nature also contradicted the scientific approaches inspired by Darwin's ideas. In 1885 Traill completed a systematic cataloguing of her beloved region of Ontario that bore her trademark layering of natural history and religious sentiment. Each element of nature had a particular place and purpose, and a 'simple history of its own . . . [forming] a page in a great volume of Nature [*sic*] . . . and without it there would be a blank – in nature there is no space left unoccupied' (Traill, *Studies of Plant Life in Canada* 1). Thus, at least two pillars of debate can be located in this glimpse of natural selection's reception in Canada. The discourse hints at Canadians' complex relationship with and attitude toward nature, which is steeped in a Linnaean method of knowing.

Late nineteenth- and early twentieth-century popular fiction writers inherited this intellectual debate and found provocative new ways in which to participate. At the turn of the twentieth century two Canadian writers were at the centre of an unlikely controversy involving the writing of children's literature. Ernest Thompson Seton led a celebrated life on both sides of the Canada-US border. In Canada, he and Charles G.D. Roberts developed a literary genre known as the realistic animal story; Seton's best known book of this sort was *Wild Animals I Have Known* (1898). His fame in the United States and Great Britain came from his founding of the Woodcraft Indian club for boys. Roberts promoted his native New Brunswick in travel literature, and was known for his popular animal stories, such as *The Kindred of the Wild: A Book of Animal Life* (1902).

Darwin's theory of evolution posed interesting, although threatening, questions for Canadians. One subset of the new theory, the ability of animals to think, as Darwin argued in *The Descent of Man* (1871), was accepted by Seton and Roberts. But the two novelists ventured onto less stable ground when they cast their lot with contemporary animal psychologists who argued that not only could animals think, they could also reason. In their texts, Seton and Roberts took the point of view of the animal. Just as the animals in the story could feel, the reader felt a sympathy for the animal. Roberts succeeded in tying 'man to the natural world but also showed him separated from it' (Dunlap, '"The Old Kinship of Earth"' 111).

Was all this simply a case of harmless, entertaining, poetic licence? John Burroughs, the most popular nature writer at the time, did not think so. The realistic animal stories ventured too far into uncharted territory, claimed Burroughs, to the point of deceiving and confusing the very audience that so loved the tales. In 1903, Burroughs publicly criticized those (including Americans Jack London and William J. Long) who purposely duped the reading public into believing that animals could reason and act like humans. The debate over 'real' versus 'sham' natural history was eventually joined by American president Theodore Roosevelt, an avid outdoorsman and admirer of Burroughs. Such stories, charged the two critics, flew in the face of all that had been constructed by writers of children's fiction to date, leaving the impression that the non-human characters had a non-verbal intellectual capacity akin to the reader. The controversy was short-lived, but it was another example of ideas in the realm of science pervading the public discourse. It would not be the last time during the twentieth century that popular writers would venture into such intellectual territory.

Conclusion

Natural resources inspired economic activity, which in turn brought local environmental changes. The most costly change in human terms was the transmission of deadly diseases that ravaged Aboriginal populations beginning around the 1630s. Natural historians were part of the great migrations from Europe and did much to explain how Canada's environments functioned. Often they pointed out the thinning animal populations and expansive forest clearances, and had the curiosity to ask whether such excesses might have long-term effects on the human condition in the colony. These sentiments would find a new and greater appreciation in coming generations as there emerged an economic, emotional, spiritual, and ecological concern for ascertaining the impact of humans on the natural world. The conservation and preservation impulses of the late nineteenth and early twentieth centuries are grounded in the questions and concerns raised by this first and early wave of natural historians.

2

Natural Resources, Economic Growth, and the Need for Conservation (1800s and 1900s)

Canada's lands and natural resources have supported both subsistence and commercial needs since the earliest Aboriginal presence. Throughout the colony, Aboriginal peoples and Euro-Canadians tapped into the abundant populations of fish and animals that existed virtually at their doorstep, accessing these resources according to the needs of individuals and communities. This 'local commons,' as American historian Louis S. Warren posits, refers to a communally regulated resource pool (Loo 15). These resources were subject to local oversight and custom and served manifold purposes: sustenance, dietary supplement, and small-scale and low-impact commercial use. In regulating the use of these resources, participants drew on local knowledge of the rhythms of nature. By no means did all users practice conservation or hold a deep, abiding love of wilderness, but practical concerns such as food gathering or supplementing annual income were paramount to their connection with their natural world.

During the nineteenth century a more elaborate network of regulations emerged to protect resources in the face of increasingly widespread uses of fish, wildlife, and forests. We might regard such conservation initiatives as affecting the 'national commons,' even though both provincial and federal governments exercised jurisdiction. These new regulations encompassed an economic use of land, forests, fisheries, and water as well as a recognition of the need to efficiently manage these elements so as to ensure future access. Incremental measures by the provincial and federal state were fuelled by a belief that such resources, inputs to production, were finite and wasted by local users. The professionalization of the sciences also impacted natural resources through the appearance of state-employed scientific managers. Allied with experts in forestry, agriculture, hydrology, fisheries biology, and the like, the state sought out approaches that would frame locally controlled resources as part of 'multiple use' programs that, for example, might include the damming of rivers to control flooding and simultaneously redistribute water to irrigate farmers' fields. Ultimately, this template favoured urban users of resources (especially anglers and hunters) over rural, local ones; in essence, it created a 'colonization' of rural space by urban dwellers (ibid. 40). As well, such schemes ostensibly presented resource management in terms of efficient and wise use meant to conserve resources into the future. Yet, as we shall see, not all programs signified such noble or seemingly class- and culturally neutral goals.

From the last third of the nineteenth century through to the Second World War, concerns over the finiteness of natural resources were being voiced. Lumbermen, commercial fishers, politicians, civil servants, scientists, and middle managers all worried that Canada's resources were being mismanaged to the point that future use might be made impossible. During this period, an effort to reorganize patterns of use, regulate forest exploitation, rationalize commercial fishing and hunting, improve public health, and promote a more efficient society ensued. There were also shared resources belonging to a 'continental commons,' which became regulated through international treaties between Canada and the United States.

Seemingly, conservation grew from an economic need for efficiency and the elimination of waste. That natural resources were so important to the economic life of the

Dominion meant that they were worth conserving. This viewpoint, as we shall see in the following chapter, differed from that of 'preservation,' which emphasised the protection of natural systems and the advent of public parks, often as ends in and of themselves. Moreover, we must recognize that conservation did not necessarily imply sustainability. The latter term would not be introduced into our vocabulary until a century later, and will be taken up in chapter four.

Finally, it is useful in setting the intellectual context of the late-Victorian age to keep the concept of vitalism in mind. As Colin Howell explains in connection with the image of a healthy body, Victorians believed that 'each individual was born with a finite amount of vital energy, which had to be carefully dispensed over the life course and not wasted in acts of physical or moral dissipation' (108–9). In other words, striking a balance between intellectual and physical activity and avoiding vices such as gluttony were central not only to individual health, but also to the well-being of society as a whole. Vitalist thinking was projected onto the natural world when middle-class Canadians considered the future economic viability of the Dominion. In sum, the conservation era was characterized by a move toward control and regulation of nature and its efficient use by citizens. The state was usually the arbiter of what was acceptable and what was not. Scientific knowledge and the state's desire to make resources and citizens conform to neat modes of use were the goals.

The Local Commons

Community and local resources mattered to Aboriginal and early non-Aboriginal populations in Canada. Custom, rather than formal statute law, decided the most essential questions, such as those regarding the amount of animals or fish taken in a given season. Indeed, in early British North America, one would be hard pressed to find legislation that sought the wise use of game, fish, and forests beyond the township, municipality, or provincial level. However, by about the mid-nineteenth century an idea developed among non-local resource users, scientists, and law makers that rural users (Aboriginal and non-Aboriginal alike) did not make good conservationists. Moreover, it was surmised that local knowledge needed to be replaced by more regulated and professionalized notions of wise use that would stem the tide of resource depletion. It is true that market hunters in parts of the United States, reacting to high prices paid for bird feathers, hunted some species into extinction. But these were rare incidents and did not accurately characterize the whole of rural people who had as much regard for their future sustenance and livelihood as anyone else.

During the nineteenth century, nearly all Aboriginal peoples were considered to be standing 'between two worlds.' The first was the traditional world guided by seasonal variations that provided a diet of fish and game, and the second was the new regime of market capitalism replete with wage labour and sedentary agriculture, which were alien to most Aboriginal people. Newcomers, as well, brought conceptions about public, communal access of natural resources that were also challenged as the century progressed. With respect to the use and protection of animals, birds, fish, and forests, the nineteenth and twentieth centuries were a period of profound change.

For both Aboriginal and non-Aboriginal peoples, the conservation of fur-bearing animals was paramount to maintaining the local commons. Even after the heyday of the fur trade faded by the dawn of the nineteenth century, furs were a valued staple. Strategies for conserving animal stocks and ensuring both subsistence and commercial uses were practiced in several subregions, but especially in the North. In the Northwest Territories, between the end of the nineteenth and early twentieth centuries, a decline in the number of muskox and caribou occurred. This was in part due to the actions of peoples (including the Dene and Inuit) supplying the meat and skin for markets in the South. Although ancillary factors including climate change and disease were certainly at play, federal agents administering the North's relationship to southern Canada reasoned that the Aboriginal hunters were the main culprits of animal depopulation. In the ensuing years, steps were taken to distance such hunters from the animals they had relied on as a resource for generations. Certain Aboriginal communities were even relocated. Scientific management was also a part of the equation as bison were moved south to populate newly established parks and thus further served to demonstrate the role of government policymakers and scientists in rearranging the natural rhythms of the North.

The HBC also played a key role in the reconsideration of Aboriginal peoples and fur staples. In the 1930s, the HBC not only sought to reinvigorate the dwindling population of beaver in Quebec's north, but also became concerned for the plight of Aboriginals whose livelihoods were intimately linked to the health of the beaver. It drew upon Cree knowledge of the animal's habits and avoided animals that were in danger of being trapped out. The program was a splendid success and became a model for such strategies. In large part, the positive results were owed to the fact that the program was decentralized and far from other would-be resource takers, but this should not detract from the success that was enjoyed by the company, the Aboriginals, and the beaver, too. All of this occurred within a slightly modified local commons wherein benefits to both the environment and society remained in place and were orchestrated by local users.

Birds also fit into the dietary and income needs of local users. These species came under increasing regulation as receptive attitudes toward state-sponsored conservation programs emerged. The public's belief that local users, if left to their own devices, would fail to manage wildfowl resources and destroy bird populations also contributed to such thinking. Local users had to be rescued from themselves. Later we will consider the 1916 Migratory Birds Convention between Canada and the United States. But first it is important to note the transition from local to national wildfowl commons. Jack Miner and his son Manly were two early proponents of a sanctuary for migratory fowl at their property in Kingsville, Ontario. Like the HBC, they practiced a type of conservation that was rooted in local knowledge and they made the effort to keep it decentralized, a philosophy that confounded government scientists such as Percy Travener who wanted more and more government oversight. The Miners provided a safe haven for birds passing through on journeys across North America and monitored their progress through a banding system. Jack especially became a conservation celebrity in his time, and the Miners' personal approach to nature conservation was well known. However, they did not follow a romantic impulse to preserve birds for their own sake. Birds, in their view, existed to serve humans, especially as natural pest controllers for the Miners' agricultural neighbours. The Miners also killed predatory crows and hawks as a way to promote what they saw as useful species such as geese and songbirds.

Local inland and coastal fishers were also confronted with change. Aboriginal peoples were left particularly vulnerable as markets emerged for a certain variety of fish, or when access to the waterways that supported aquatic life were appropriated for other uses such as tourism. Nevertheless, they clung to the fishery as a source of sustenance and income (for instance, by becoming guides for sportsmen in the East or workers in BC canneries).

One of the most systematic examples of the colonization of local resources can be found on the salmon rivers of Eastern Canada. The Mi'kmaq, for instance, used spears to capture salmon, especially with the aid of torch lights during the spring and summer months; they had employed these means of capture since before colonial times. The introduction of European peoples to the Atlantic region through the eighteenth century and the advent of a prosperous timber economy in New Brunswick during the nineteenth century placed population and pollution pressures on the salmon rivers of the region. Mill refuse, dammed passage ways, and overfishing with nets had so imperilled the fishery that three provinces on the Atlantic seaboard – New Brunswick (1851), Nova Scotia (1853), and Quebec (1857) – enacted laws to toughen already existing (but rarely enforced) statutes. In so doing, New Brunswick legislators added language outlawing certain means of capture that the Mi'kmaq and other Aboriginals used, such as spearing or the setting of nets during spawning season. Aboriginal peoples now faced prosecution for transgressions of the new laws. Effectively cut off from the harvesting of salmon, and faced with possible starvation for want of wage labour, some Aboriginals turned to the sport-fishing industry as guides.

'Primitive' means of capture like spearing infuriated the new class of gentlemen sportsmen, who were critical not only of what they regarded as wastefulness in the case of large harvests, but also what they deemed the lack of Aboriginal skill and dexterity. Anglers fashioned themselves as the inheritors of Isaac Walton's philosophy. He was the Scottish author of the *Compleat Angler* (1653), and advocated a code of fair play between the sport fisher and his would-be catch. Urban sportsmen saw themselves as both social arbiters and protectors of the 'code of the sportsman.' Moreover, the sportsmen led the charge at the provincial level, pressuring assemblies to pass hunting and fishing (more properly, angling) codes throughout the nineteenth century. The nascent tourist industry was complicit with the regional railways. These railways could bring weary urbanites, their nerves frazzled by the demands of the modern era, to the wilds of Canada in a matter of hours – in the comfort of sleeper cars.

Indeed, railway travel was part of this new trend toward leisure activity among the North American elite. Once arriving at their destination, travellers would find accommodation with local hotels that provide the transition into the sporting life. Anglers supported controversial hatchery programs, which necessitated the leasing of land and stretches of river to private sporting clubs that paid tens of thousands of dollars annually to foster the artificial propagation of salmon. Clubs employed local guardians to protect against poachers. One group alone, the Restigouche Salmon Club, spent more than $5,000 in 1890 to protect its leasehold.

Non-Aboriginals, too, experienced the onset of fisheries regulations that more often than not advantaged the burgeoning tourist industry of the late nineteenth and early twentieth centuries. For instance, as a sporting fraternity grew in North America and sought the prized Atlantic salmon of Eastern Canada, it bought exclusive leases to New Brunswick and Quebec rivers that barred local users from the resource that many considered their birth right to catch. The purchase of the lease obligated the sporting clubs to hire guardians to police their holdings. Moreover, the method of capture, from the use of nets to the use of only a fly, further angered the predominantly rural population that supplemented annual diets or sold the annually migrating fish as a means of making money. Sporting clubs, as in the United States during the same period, were exclusive; locals would be hired only to safeguard the enjoyment these men sought when they ventured to the wilds in search of relaxation, adventure, camaraderie, and a chance to demonstrate their skill with the fly rod.

Conservation policies could also be read as social policies. The reform of Canada's social ills was an underlying message of moves to strengthen the hand of governments, while the science community was increasingly accorded domain over the natural world. Throughout the country from the mid-nineteenth century to about the 1930s, laws were passed that excluded local users in favour of (often urban) sportsmen who desired plentiful game and fish. Sportsmen also relished the thought of spending a period in the woods and reclaiming the manly pursuits that some social commentators believed they were losing. One such voice, in 1897, offered that '[w]e are as a people living at too rapid a rate; we are in the eager scramble for wealth and position.' Sporting seemed the cure for 'overworked business men' and they should be encouraged

to take an interest in such employment as the rod and gun will furnish. Anything that will lead them out into the woods and fields is to be commended . . . it will be upon this that the future longevity, the vitality of the race will depend. (Forkey, 'Anglers, Fishers, and the St Croix River' 181)

Recalling the vitalist message, these same participants would have seen a foray into the pursuits of their forefathers as a means of regenerating a society whose middle class was sapped of the sorts of benefits that fresh air and sporting activity could offer.

The management of the ocean and inland fisheries passed into the federal domain with Confederation. Provinces, however, still legislated usage and treatment of streams. Under the rubric of 'rehabilitation, regulation, and enforcement' the federal government in 1868 adopted a fisheries protection law similar to ones in effect in Ontario and Quebec since the 1850s. Pisciculture formed an important pillar of the new act, as did the digging of channels to allow fish to pass through saw mill refuse. On the latter point, the government pressured mill owners to stop the practice of polluting streams. Fishing was banned on certain overfished rivers, a move condoned by sportsmen. In order to ensure that the new regulations were obeyed, wardens were appointed to police the waterways. In the early 1880s, New Brunswick and Quebec regained control over the leasing of rivers; spurred by the lucrative nature of the sporting economy, legislators catered to the outside travellers that so promoted the region's economy. Nova Scotia followed suit; there, policy was also strongly influenced by this elite group who appeared to be guiding legislative action.

Local users, however, did not acquiesce so easily. Often bands of four to five men ignored the regulations and caught salmon on several area rivers and at the head of tide. Along the Saguenay and Ste Marguerite Rivers in Quebec, the Wallace in Nova Scotia, the Dunk in Prince Edward Island, and the Miramichi and Restigouche in New Brunswick, poaching became a significant problem. In the most extreme cases, the property of overseers in Quebec and New Brunswick was torched as a means of intimidation or to exact vengeance for the confiscation of fishing nets. One tragic encounter involved the 1888 shooting death of a Massachusetts woman vacationing with her family on the Tobique River in New Brunswick by two men later charged as poachers. The men received fifteen-year prison sentences after a jury trial. Indeed, these types of encroachments upon local resources in the effort to turn a provincial profit distanced rural people from the fish and wildlife that they had always regarded as common property. Such cases stand as testimony to the fact that conservation laws, superficially noble gestures to defend nature, were highly charged exercises in which urban/rural, rich/poor, recreational/commercial, and Canadian/Aboriginal divides often emerged.

Aboriginal peoples also attempted to enter the commercial fisheries as labourers, a means of coping with this new political economy. The Ojibwa of Northern Ontario were active in that region. They advocated for better protection of their (and the province's) resources. Whitefish and sturgeon were taken by Ojibwa and Minnesota fishers in waterways connected to the Lake of the Woods and on the Rainy River; although the former had done so since before the completion of Treaty Three in 1873, the latter had done so only since 1884. In agreeing to the treaty, the Ojibwa had essentially agreed to share the resources since there was ample evidence to suggest that whitefish and sturgeon were standards of their diet. The Department of Marine and Fisheries licenced Canadian fishers, as did the state of Minnesota with Americans. Yet, the licences seemed to do more harm than good. By 1892, eleven chiefs charged that non-Aboriginal fishers were doing irreparable harm to the common resources, so much so that the Ojibwa found 'one of [their] main resources [getting] more and more scarce and [they could] now hardly catch enough to feed [themselves] in summertime' (Van West 32). Yet, the chiefs were arguing a lost cause as both Canadian and American fisheries overseers proved ineffective – the continued exploitation of the fishery ultimately paved the way to its collapse by 1915.

The Pacific Coast offers a similar story. After British Columbia's entry into Confederation in 1871 the salmon fishery that had existed prior to that period took on a new importance in the local economies of both Aboriginals and whites. Regulation that had been previously nonexistent was introduced. An exchange network was in place whereby Aboriginals traded with newcomers (usually American mariners) and salmon was a central ingredient. Under the new regime, however, Aboriginals were expected to fish for subsistence and not engage the market, a move designed to keep supplies of fish more abundant for the non-Aboriginal commercial fishers. While an Aboriginal fishery in the commercial age did emerge, it was soon eclipsed as Natives sought wage labour in the canneries. This change was all the more facilitated as the federal government brought in conservation measures such as a licencing system and put restrictions on certain means of capture such as the Aboriginal-preferred weirs that sat at the mouths of salmon rivers.

For peoples whose cultures were so wedded to the fish, this was surely a difficult transition, although one they did not undergo without a fight. The Cowichan experience with federal conservation law provides a revealing glimpse into the complexity of the BC situation. By the late 1870s, the Aboriginals formed the backbone of the BC salmon fishing industry and their weirs netted abundant harvests that were shared by the whole community. In 1885, the Department of Marine and Fisheries enacted laws that left open the weirs during weekends. The Department was not overly concerned that the weirs alone could deplete the resource; however, officials reasoned that in tandem with growing white-owned fishing fleets and viewed over the long term, the situation could prove ruinous for the province's economy. In 1894, the law was amended to protect salmon spawning beds (precisely where the weirs were located) and effectively halted the taking of fish. In addition to the canneries' demand for salmon, a tourist trade was emerging and well-stocked rivers were the major attraction for sportsmen. The Cowichan opposed the new regulations and continued to fish with weirs. A year later, the principal violators were on trial in federal court. The case demonstrated a crucial new reality for both Aboriginals and the state apparatus designed to care for them on the reserves: if the Cowichan could not take fish for subsistence, then they would have to turn to the Department of Indian Affairs for support, a prospect that did not interest the government. Fisheries overseers showed leniency in enforcing the regulations, and in fact, white missionaries and others from the newcomer communities agreed with the Cowichan's defence, some even pointing out that the weirs were less dangerous than imagined by the fishery regulators. The Cowichan, like other BC Aboriginal groups, began to see their sources of food and cash remade to fit the prevailing economic mode and the legal apparatus that supported it. By the early twentieth century some pointedly expressed the way they perceived themselves in this new reality, stating, '[i]n many places we are debarred from camping, traveling, gathering roots . . . [and] our people are fined and imprisoned for breaking the game and fish laws . . . [g]radually we are becoming regarded as trespassers over a large portion of this country' (Thoms 98). What is crucial to recognize in these cases, however, is that Aboriginal peoples did not passively watch control of their resources slip through their fingers. They frequently sounded the clarion call for wiser resource-protection measures, but most importantly they did so in ways that elevated the supremacy of the local commons.

A sea change was also evident as social reformers sought to promote an image of law and order in one of Canada's most important industrial cities: Hamilton (Burlington Bay). As we saw in the case of the Eastern Seaboard, the mid-nineteenth century marked the dawn of fishery laws that sought to edge non-licenced fishers out of business, in favour of commercial fishers and sport anglers. During the 1860s, John William Kerr, a former constable from County Fermanagh, Ireland, emerged as a strict enforcer of local and provincial laws that served to oust working-class 'poachers' from disturbing what some elites in Hamilton envisioned as a preserve for sportsmen. One of the means of capture that Kerr objected to, for instance, was the spearing of fish through the ice during winter, an Aboriginal practice that went back generations and that the working classes had taken up. The surveillance of poachers had as much to do with regulating behaviour in a city that was a destination for working-class immigrants as it did with conservation. Hamiltonian boosters sought to uplift the working poor of Burlington Heights and Dundas Marsh, those who lived in a boathouse colony along the waterfront. The shanties were the bane of reformers who believed that they were not only unsightly for a burgeoning tourist trade, but also the sign of a social class in the grip of moral decay who were likely to partake in heavy drinking, gambling, and blood sports. For these reasons, a successful campaign was waged between 1920 and 1940 to dismantle the boathouse community. Thus, conservation could mean quite different things for the acquisition and use of resources depending upon one's place in the social hierarchy.

Even in the arena of forests, the local commons were being changed. Aboriginals in Ontario and the Rockies found themselves excluded from the commons to make way for parks. The prevailing attitude among parks planners, not unlike what we have seen above, was that Aboriginals would take fish and game out of season, not only going against the idea of a pristine park, but, more to the point, disrupting the tourist economies that were linked to these spaces. The exclusion of Aboriginals from such sought-after locations as Point Pelee and Georgian Bay Islands National Parks in Ontario and the even more touted Rocky Mountains (Banff) National Park in Alberta represented a last attempt to push Aboriginals to the margins in order to remake the 'natural' landscape to suit the needs and tastes of late-Victorian Canada. The shift toward creating a national commons was underway.

The National Commons

National commons refers to the way in which Canada's natural and human resources were envisioned in the broadest possible sense. Science played a major role in the resource management schemes. The state tapped information generated by the physical sciences to conserve species, but also to augment nature's productive capacity and add to the national wealth generated by resource exploitation. Multiple-use projects such as the damming of rivers to create hydroelectricity, irrigate fields, or lessen the severity of floods were part of the strategy.

By bounding the land, cultivating new crops, grazing livestock, encouraging population growth, and providing the impetus for both subsistence and commercial agriculture, Europeans brought profound physical changes to Canada. Although this equation was infused with notions of private property and the chance to impart land to successive generations, clearly what was emerging after Confederation was a national commons in the sense that Canadians relied upon one another for survival. Elements of the land, especially forests, were crucial to this sense of shared national resources. What followed the consolidation of the local commons was what we might consider the start of efficiently managing natural resources and, in no small way, society too. In various ways farmland, forests, and waters became a subject for social commentators, policymakers, and the public as late nineteenth century populations grew and questions arose about the finiteness of resources and the quality of Canadian life. Urban and rural settings were put under greater scrutiny as questions of public health became more prominent. Scientific management of resources was also a feature of this period, although, as we shall see, social and cultural perceptions still coloured the way in which supposedly objective-minded practitioners pursued their subjects.

No other resource mattered more under this new rubric than Crown forests. The Maritimes and Central Canada had been focal points in the extraction and sale of timber in Europe and the United States for earlier generations. New technologies after the mid-nineteenth century such as the steam-powered saw and locomotive accelerated the pace of exploitation into the early twentieth century. Continental rail lines further eased the ability of US markets to consume Canadian timber. The railways themselves were yet another means by which those same trees were put into manifold production. The 1885 completion of the CPR was a milestone. It spanned nearly five thousand kilometres and required two thousand wooden ties for every kilometre of track; in turn, these needed to be replaced every three to four years. Wooden bridges (the largest requiring two million board feet of milled timber), telegraph lines, boxcars, stations, and roundhouses supported the industry. Ironically, locomotives (with wood- and coal-burning furnaces) and the cars they pulled along steel rails were prime spark arresters and frequently ignited fires in the forests through which they passed. In Ontario's north it was lamented that

[f]rom Sudbury to Port Arthur, generally speaking, the country along the [Algoma Central] railway has been burned at one time or another for the entire distance of 550 miles. Not much has escaped except the spruce swamps. The burned areas have been

partially recovered by temporary stands of poplar, white birch and jack pine, either pure or in mixture. But to a vast extent the country has been burned so repeatedly that there is nothing left but bare rock. (Drushka 37)

Railways enabled settlement in most parts of North America during the latter third of the nineteenth century. As populations increased so too did demand for homes and other wood-produced goods. Canadian forests were in high demand; the 1873 value of Canadian lumber exports to the United States was $9.5 million, a number that rose to $150 million by 1920. As Atlantic and Central Canadian forests were thinned and pulp and paper production became the primary concerns, British Columbia's forests took on greater importance vis-à-vis the American market. The CPR's completion aided this trend, as more and better access to and from mills was assured. In 1885, coastal mills annually cut 75 million board feet; by 1906, that amount reached 525 million board feet.

In the second half of the nineteenth century concerns were voiced about the pace of forest extraction. As early as 1862, John Langton, a long-time resident, lumber entrepreneur, and politician around Peterborough, Ontario, decried the indiscriminate felling of young trees that were then left to rot on the ground and fuel forest fires. He also criticized the wasteful cutting practices that came from squaring timber (whereby he estimated that 20 per cent of the best part of the tree was chipped away). Langton also warned that settlement on timber berths of the Canadian Shield (with its hard rock and thin soils), in the region north of Lake Ontario and between Ottawa and Lake Huron, was pure folly; these parcels could never support farm families. He preferred instead a designation of such lands for lumbering, an early expression of the 'forest reserve' idea. 'Where the land is of such quality as to support an agricultural population,' Langton articulated, by all means let the settlement proceed as rapidly as possible, for with all my respect for timber, I value a man more than a great many trees. But a very large portion of our back country never can maintain a healthy settlement. The cheapness of the land, and ignorance of what can be profitably worked [attract many would-be settlers, who] destroy much [of the forest], and the lumberer who has a license over the land, when he finds the settlers approaching, has to scramble for anything he can get, before it passes out of his hands, to the destruction of any well-organized plan of making the most of his [leased] limits. (75)

Policymakers in North America were especially taken with the ideas expressed by the American George Perkins Marsh. The publication of Marsh's *Man and Nature: Or, Physical Geography as Modified by Human Action* (1864), with its alarming message that forests, often the strength of many a great empire, were being ruinously treated, struck a chord among Canadians. One of these Canadians was James Little, who had made his fortune as a lumberman. Echoing the views of both Langton and Marsh, he called for the protection of quality timber stands and government intervention to classify lands for farming and lumbering. Little supported the notion of forest reserves and reforestation, and heaped blame upon Crown lands timber administrators who put too many acres into production without recognizing the consequences of overcutting. He charged that 'this reprehensible course has been the means of stimulating production to such an extent that the greatest and most shameful waste of this indispensable material has become the order of the day' (Little 4). Little denounced such practices as contributing to a 'national suicide' (ibid. 5).

It is not surprising then that the earliest voices favouring forest conservation came from the industry itself. When the American Forestry Association was organized in 1875, for example, the group attracted interested Canadian lumbermen. In fact, the Association's 1882 meeting was held in Montreal, in large part due to this enthusiasm. The Canadian Forestry Association was founded in 1900 by Sir Henri-Gustave Joly de Lotbinière, a largescale landowner from Quebec who had successfully tested European forestry techniques on his own forest holdings. During his long career in public service, he served as lieutenant-governor of British Columbia, where he introduced conservation measures. The Association's members came from the ranks of business, civil service, and especially science; the body promoted conservation measures and the creation of a forestry school.

The Prussian-trained Bernhard E. Fernow was among the most influential members of this rising class of scientific foresters. Indeed, he earned fame as an educator at numerous North American universities during the late nineteenth and early twentieth centuries. He established the Faculty of Forestry at the University of Toronto in 1903, and became its dean in 1907; among one of the earliest graduates of the program was Judson F. Clark, the first official forester employed in Canada. Fernow left his mark on future policy planning, as his students carried forth his ideas on forest replanting, selective harvesting (which included the fixing of diameter limits below which trees could not be cut), the scrupulous marking of trees to be felled so as not to damage others, and the beginning of sustained-yield growth models. Among other things, he articulated the need for studies in soil and water conservation, paleobotany (the study of fossil plants), mycology (the study of fungi), entomology (the study of insects), ecology, and kindred topics. Although Fernow was entering new territory in the study of silviculture (the growing and cultivation of trees), clearly his message was also in keeping with the political economy of the Canadian forests. An investment in conservation today meant forests that could be used tomorrow. Indeed, Ontario and Quebec were already experimenting with an idea that emerged from this North American preoccupation with the health of the woodlands: forest reserves. In important ways, the forest reserves served as the basis for the provincial and national parks, as they purposely set aside lands for specific uses.

Attempts at a conservation agenda came in similar ways to the forests of British Columbia. There, lumberers descended upon the Douglas fir forests beginning in 1858, the same year that gold was discovered on the Fraser River. This rush-to-riches atmosphere ushered in a period when newcomers regarded BC as a place to turn 'trees into dollars' (Hak 5). The land had no value, it was presumed, until a staple product could be found. By the 1890s critics such as Dr Hugh Watt, a member of the Legislative Assembly from Cariboo, raised concerns about the lack of forest regulation. Watt insisted upon rational planning in the cutting of forests and replanting of the species that were most heavily culled. Most of all, however, he refuted the popular belief so prevalent to the end of the century that the BC forests were inexhaustible. A moral imperative informed his message as he argued against the squandering of resources to the disadvantage of future generations: 'we are but temporary trustees,' he reminded, 'of the land and its resources' (ibid. 93). As well, he drew a parallel between the health of the forests and the prospects for future revenues from tourism. He surmised that if forests became denuded and fish and game suffered, BC would no longer exist as a sporting paradise. Watt called for state supervision of the forests, monitored logging practices, and a regulated cut of timber that spared young trees during the annual harvest. However, in a decentralized economy where a combination of large- and small-scale lumber firms vied for the treasures of the forests, the provincial regulations that Watt desired remained elusive.

Regulation was so elusive that into the next decade the escapades of rapacious lumbermen were fictionalized in popular literature. M. Allerdale Grainger, a civil servant turned author, used the working forest to showcase the gritty world of unchecked human avarice. In so doing, he roundly critiqued the practices of so-called 'siwash loggers' who worked within a thousand feet of the coast, cutting only the trees that could be easily hauled out and destroying other stands in the process, and who were entirely ignorant of selective cutting schemes. Of his fictional lumber boss he wrote,

[m]uch he cared that he was spoiling leases for future working, like a mine manager who should hurriedly exhaust the rich patches of his mine. Leases, he said, were going up in value. Some one would find it worth while some day to buy from him the stretches of forest whose sea-fronts he had shattered and left in tangled wreckage. As for him, he was going to butcher his woods as he pleased. It paid! (Grainger 77)

Grainger did more than simply craft an exposé of the inefficiency at hand in BC's forests. He used his knowledge of such practices in his later position as secretary of a provincial royal commission on foresting and went on to write the report that led to the British Columbia Forest Act of 1912, which (among other things) created a professional forestry branch from which conservation strategies could be pursued (although they rarely were). Grainger would also serve as BC's chief forester between 1917 and 1920. All told, forest conservation legislation for much of the twentieth century failed to protect BC's forest in the ways that Watt, Grainger, and successive figures would have liked. So important to the provincial economy were private lumbering companies (especially in the first half of the century), that provincial governments hesitated to strictly enforce legislation that safeguarded forests.

Studies conducted between 1890 and 1910 at McGill University contributed to ensuring the health of Canada's forests. Scientists there sought to understand and perhaps enhance the durability of certain species. These studies began in an atmosphere of utilitarianism. Sir John William

Dawson elicited funding from Montreal's business community. The idea was to select, based on laboratory investigation, the best species for economic use and leave those deemed less desirable. In 1891, Henry Taylor Bovey, a Devonshire-born engineer, helped to create in Montreal a program that would test the elastic limit, or maximum stress that materials could endure without damage. Thus a meeting of engineering and botany was effected, the latter personified by David Pearce Penhallow. Program members chose firs, pines, and tamaracks from the same vicinity in BC and subjected them to the Wicksteed strength-testing machine, a hundred-ton machine designed to assess the quality of construction materials. The trees were hauled across the country by the CPR and made available for analysis. The hydraulic-powered Wicksteed strained twenty-four-foot trees until they snapped, thus measuring the stress that they could withstand. These torture-chamber-like feats aided researchers in understanding which conifer and other species were most desirable for the lumberers to collect and which to disregard and leave standing.

As well, studies of live and fossilized trees, it was hoped, would yield data about their life cycles and origins. In applying a post-Darwinian scientific method, Penhallow was instrumental in probing the anatomy of the trees; for example, the vascular systems within the cross-section of the trunk. He then compared certain fossilized specimens and concluded that the conifers (*Coniferales*) evolved from an extinct species of tree shared by others such as monkey puzzles (*Araucaria*) and gingkoes (*Gingkoales*). As the genealogical line extended to the contemporary period, it passed to families of yew, redwood, cedar, cypress, fir, hemlock, Douglas fir, larch, and spruce. Ultimately, this lineage culminated with the pine, which he considered the most complex and resinous of the forest. Susan Zeller makes the point that Penhallow 'imagined the conifers' evolution as a finite process of descent through a series of lateral members' (438). In other words, Penhallow discerned an ongoing, evolving process that suggested the forest was not a relic, but was the result of a history that worked toward a more perfect end. Coupled with the strength tests, the plotting of the pine's lineage served the interests not only of science, but also those enlightened lumbermen and conservationists who desired to reap only those species that were strong and economically valuable while doing as little harm to the overall forest as possible.

The state and science were also wedded to the cause of conserving aquatic species. During the second half of the nineteenth century commercial fishing in the international Great Lakes drainage basin boomed. Urban transhipment centres emerged at Detroit, Toronto, Chicago, Buffalo, Cleveland, and Sandusky, Ohio. Activities increased throughout the period without much critical analysis of questions of supply, demand, and method of shipment. In 1872, a report issued by Illinois biologist James Milner for the US Fish and Fisheries Commission tracked the growth of the industry that had turned Canadian and American Great Lakes operations into a $1.8 million annual concern. The report suggested that activities were grand, and becoming grander: Canadians claimed over seven million pounds of fish per year, while Americans claimed more than thirty-two million. Fishers were becoming outfitted with more efficient technology in nets and boats, processing facilities were more heavily capitalized, and marketing and distribution were heightened as the reach of lake steamers and railways more quickly than ever made Great Lakes fish an international commodity. The addition of the refrigerated boxcar in the 1870s only increased the ability of large dealers like the Alfred Booth Packing Company of Chicago to access many American cities whose working-class populations had developed appetites for the seemingly plentiful and often inexpensive nutritional whitefish. But how stable was the fishery? No one knew for certain, and few fishers, dealers, or others in the supply and delivery ends of the operations asked such a question. Individual incomes hinged upon the ability to catch more and more fish, and dealers (who owned the means of production and sometimes the boats used by fishers) sought to drive hard bargains at the expense of their labourers in the interest of turning a profit. This situation continued until the 1890s when downturns in the amount of fish caught were recognized. The prized whitefish catches declined precipitously in all five Great Lakes plus Lake St Clair during a twenty-year period, from over twenty-four thousand pounds in 1879 to a mere nine thousand pounds by 1899. Overfishing was one cause, but loss of habitat due to pollution from cities and urban industrial growth that altered water tables and increased soil run-off from the depleted forests around the basin were also likely reasons for the plummeting catches.

Throughout this period, American and Canadian fishery experts attempted to correct the declining numbers by tinkering with the natural cycle of whitefish and other species. At this time, pisciculture was more a 'practical' than a 'pure' science. Practitioners believed that overfishing was the cause of catch declines and thus reasoned that artificially propagating more fish and then releasing them into the resource pool would remedy the problem. They were proved incorrect. Ancillary variables such as habitat loss and pollution also had to be taken into account, and were not. Nonetheless, Ontario's Samuel Wilmot experimented with hatching stations throughout the lower Canadian Great Lakes, especially at Newcastle, Sandwich, and briefly on the Bay of Quinte. Although Quebec's superintendent of fisheries Richard Nettle had first experimented with artificial propagation in the 1850s, it was Wilmot at his Newcastle facility that, beginning in 1867, moved the idea to the practical stage. The Dominion government began underwriting his operations at Newcastle, the first such facility in North America. Here, he took the eggs of female whitefish and mixed them with the milt of the male. The fertilized eggs were enclosed in trays and troughs and incubated for six months, after which time they hatched. When the fry attained the weight of one pound, they were released into open water. Throughout his career

Wilmot was recognized internationally as an expert in the field and moved through the ranks of the Department of Marine and Fisheries, becoming the superintendent of fish culture in 1876.

During the first third of the twentieth century, the creation of a national commons also meant the re-engineering of rivers, mainly for hydroelectric power development. The scenario occurred in most provinces, but three case studies from Northern Ontario, Quebec's Saguenay region, and BC's Fraser River are illustrative; an example from Alberta's Bow River will be taken up more thematically in the next chapter.

At the start of the twentieth century, Ontario looked to its north to further exploit forests and minerals. It was imagined that settlement in 'New Ontario' would mimic the course of industry, and that other locales on this resource frontier would follow the success of Sudbury (where nickel was mined) and Kirkland Lake (important for gold). Such energy-intensive endeavours required a steady and inexpensive supply of electrical current; to furnish this, private and provincial dams were erected. One such project was launched along the Mattagami and Abitibi Rivers systems, which empty into the Ontario side of James Bay. These were ancestral lands of the Cree and Anishnabe peoples who, for generations, travelled upon the waterways that fronted their homes and subsisted on local fish and wildfowl. Early in the twentieth century, the federal government negotiated for these lands, and soon Ontario's northern boundary was extended to give the province ownership of the land. Once these rivers were dammed, however, the local environment changed. The pickerel and sturgeon fisheries declined. The water table was altered so that some poplar stands were flooded and the beaver dispersed (thus eliminating a source of food and an element of the cash economy with the HBC). In other areas, dams slowed the water to a perpetual low ebb, causing traditional beaver trap lines to wallow in the mud for lack of current. Inequities in water levels also prevented easy portages from one community to another. Even the simple act of wild berry picking was rendered impossible. Finally, in an extreme case, Mattagami Indian Reserve #71 became flooded when water was stored on the reserve, thus forcing the relocation of an entire community.

In Quebec, the quest to possess and put to use the thundering flow of the Saguenay River became the vision of American industrialist and waterpower developer James B. Duke. The idea was to create a reliable energy supply for heavy industry such as aluminum refining, and to propel more local concerns such as pulp and paper manufacturing by damming the Saguenay and storing water in Lac Saint-Jean. The Quebec government was by no means hostile to the project, which, if successful, might provide employment to residents of this remote area of the province. The grandiose scheme can easily be seen as an instrument of public policy designed to keep the population from joining other out-migrants from the province. In the words of the premier, Louis-Alexandre Taschereau, on the eve of the commencement of the project, 'there is a dream [long embraced by the premier and his predecessors]: the construction of a dam on the great inland sea Lac Saint-Jean which, for centuries, has let a million horsepower daily run to waste' (Massell 4). He also hoped that this mythic powerhouse would, 'create such centres of industry that those of our young people who don't hear the call of the farm or of the liberal professions, might find jobs, instead of immigrating in search of work to the United States' (ibid.). Work began on the project in the winter of 1923 and by the summer of 1926 a large dam had been constructed at Isle Maligne. According to its chief engineer, it was 'the largest single installation in waterpower development ever undertaken . . . the eighth wonder of the world' (ibid. 5). Duke and his engineers delivered on their promise to electrify the distant region: upon its completion, the dam was making 657,000 horsepower available to the long-situated Price

Brothers pulp and paper concerns, and hydroelectricity was transmitted to the city of Quebec. Simultaneously, the Aluminum Company of America (Alcoa) contracted for power and made arrangements to construct a larger powerhouse.

In the post-World War I era, this sort of direct American investment in the Canadian economy was desired by capitalists and the Quebec government; however, local farmers and residents bore the brunt of the impact of such large-scale altering of water tables, which had until that point remained intact since the glacial age. The project had not been devised in a wilderness, free of human habitation. The region had been populated by individuals from the Quebec-Charlevoix region to the south beginning in the mid-nineteenth century. A railway link by 1888 had spurred further demographic growth, and despite the short growing season, agriculture was a mainstay of local livelihoods. The project necessitated raising the water level in the lake seventeen-and-a-half feet above the normal low watermark. Consequently, over twelve thousand acres of farmland would be inundated, and about 350 farmers would be detached from their sources of food and income. While farmers near the banks of the river would be flooded, those that counted on the source from upstream would be deprived of water to irrigate their fields. As monopoly capitalism arrived in the Saguenay region, local people were agitated over 'la tragédie du Lac Saint-Jean' (ibid. 195). From 1915 to the start of construction, local farmers circulated petitions that sought at least a compromise wherein development could exist alongside agriculture. The petitioners also feared that because the lake's ice discharge would be annually blocked in spring, the region would become chilled and threaten the already short span of annual agricultural potential. 'Who has made the region what it is?' they implored, '[w]ho is master of the soil and of the weather? . . . Why change the order of things for the profit of a few foreigners and to the detriment of the deserving class? . . . Why not at least build the dam lower and satisfy the two parties?' they asked (ibid. 132). However eloquent and impassioned their message, the issue was a dead letter. The dam went ahead, and the flooded lands were not purchased outright from the farmers when the flood gates were closed. The region became linked not only to the national commons but to the global economy. Aluminum production only increased in this region, especially during the Second World War, when Alcoa filled defence contracts for the Allied war effort.

Like the eastern waterways, British Columbia's Fraser River was also impacted by economic development. There Pacific salmon faced threats as hydroelectric development emerged as a principal concern of the twentieth century. Some locations were renowned for their enormous seasonal runs of the salmon that, for generations before Euro-Canadian settlement, had been a staple of Aboriginal communities such as the Nlaka'pamux (Thompson Indians) and the Salish. The introduction of the Canadian Pacific and Canadian National railways to the region between the 1880s and 1910s prompted improvements that allowed the cars to traverse the Fraser. In the wake of construction, rock slides followed at a section of the river known as Hell's Gate, especially after dynamite was used. The alterations corrupted the passageways that the adult salmon normally accessed at spawning season. In time, the water level around Hell's Gate dropped by fifteen feet. This jeopardized the lucrative commercial fishery that thrived downriver in Puget Sound, the only one of the large cannery sites that persisted as a mainstay of the BC economy. This fact, coupled with low consumer demand for electricity, forced stakeholders to reconsider the further development of the lower Fraser River. Smaller dams were constructed but never to the detriment of the salmon fishery. In this particular case, user rights were balanced against one another.

The transition from local to national commons was gradual and resulted from incremental policy shifts at the provincial and federal levels. The state's desire to reorient Canadian society along what it believed to be a more efficient and homogenous path is exemplified through the Commission of Conservation (1909–21). The idea for a

Canadian body to promote conservationist thought sprang from a 1909 conference in Washington, DC, that included Canadian and Mexican representatives. The desire to rationalize resource use was the driving force behind the Commission, and it established a veritable clearinghouse for conservation thought. However, it could only make recommendations; it had no force of law. The length and breadth of the Commission's interests was impressive, and during its evanescent twelve-year existence it investigated topics including fisheries conservation, oyster culturing, the creation of model forests and other silviculture ventures, fur farming, meteorology, water pollution, coal mining, rural planning, agricultural improvements, and urban fire protection. It was as concerned with natural resources as it was with social reform, and often regarded these issues as intertwined.

Interestingly, the Commission's chairman was Sir Clifford Sifton, who had shaped land and settlement policies as Sir Wilfrid Laurier's Minister of the Interior and Immigration. In inaugurating the Commission in 1910, Sifton warned his listeners that the conservation of the country's resources was essential if Canada were to continue along its prosperous path. He insisted that

if . . . we are desirous that Canada [remain] . . . a good place for our children to make their homes, it is in the highest degree important that we should endeavour to promote such improvements in the organic laws of the country as will prevent the monopolization of the sources of wealth. (Canada, Commission of Conservation 26)

For Sifton the Commission was just the defensive instrument the country needed, and should be embraced by Canadians, for it served as 'the embodiment of public spirit and advanced thought' that could channel the idea of a national commons to fruition. In such a scenario, science – not local custom – could inform the public notion of efficient use. To put an even finer point on this idea, Sifton in 1914 declared that public health was a central pillar of the Commission's work, and that while it was 'important to . . . conserve all those natural resources from which man derives his livelihood, it was still more important that the efficiency of the human unit, the health and the happiness and the vigour of the individual, should be preserved' (Sifton 214). This sentiment meshed well with the mission of the body, and was especially prevalent in its journal, *The Conservation of Life*. Here, readers could find articles on many topics that related to urban problems; titles included 'Disinfection of Shaving Brushes,' 'National Committee for Combating Venereal Disease,' and 'Maternal Nursing of Children.'

The Commission was not breaking entirely new ground on such a social reform front. Concern about the health and well-being of Canadians was a characteristic of the late-Victorian era, and was often manifested in the messages of those worried by Canada's steadily urbanized nature. Rural areas were losing population to cities, and in the minds of some, immigration from places other than the traditional British Isles sources threatened to weaken the social fabric that had been woven for many decades. Nearly 3 million Canadians lived in rural areas in 1871, compared to about 720,000 urban dwellers. By 1891 that ratio was 3.3 million rural dwellers to 1.5 million urban dwellers; by 1931 the urban population (5.6 million) had eclipsed the rural (4.8 million). Montreal, Toronto, Winnipeg, and Vancouver experienced the largest growth. Ghettos within the cities were common as immigrants and rural migrants sought employment and housing. This growth, however, came with a downside. Social reformers from various backgrounds decried the spread of disease, poverty, and crime that was not new to Canadian cities, but was now being experienced on a larger scale. The construction of sanitary water and sewage systems were among the responses of urban administrators in Montreal, Calgary, and Vancouver during this period. Moreover, city planning became included in long-term visions for the improved health, cleanliness, and order of urban life. It was with these goals in mind that Thomas

Adams joined the Commission of Conservation in 1914 as an advisor on town planning. Adams was influential in lobbying provincial legislatures to regulate suburban expansion. In 1916, for example, he helped to organize the Civic Improvement League for Canada. This consolidated interest at the federal level facilitated an international response for the protection of resources.

The Continental Commons

Canada's natural resources are by no means exclusively Canadian. Aquatic species, birds, and animals migrate across the Canada-US border annually. The rise of both nation-states during the nineteenth and twentieth centuries gave rise to the necessity of jointly managing such resources, especially in the domains of water and air quality. Because such natural elements were (and still are) valued by citizens on both sides of the international boundary, it became incumbent upon the federal states to craft agreements that protected these resources into the future. While this is clearly an illustration of the economic emphasis accorded to natural resources in the two countries, it is worth underscoring the diplomatic achievements of Ottawa and Washington over the past century. In no small way, the cordial relations and successful agreements achieved between these neighbouring countries have made them a model for other nations hoping to strike bilateral agreements regarding their shared environments. The Boundary Waters Treaty of 1909, which created the International Joint Commission (IJC), stands as a globally admired example of environmental diplomacy.

As we have seen, the late nineteenth to the early twentieth century was a period in both Canada and the United States when social issues were on the minds of middle-class reformers who pressured elected officials to pass legislation affecting such issues as food safety and other public health concerns. This era of progressive reform resulted in treaties between Canada and the United States for the protection of migratory species claimed by both countries, such as seals and birds.

Take, for example, the case of pelagic seals born on the American-claimed Pribilof Islands, off the Alaska coast. The United States claimed permanent ownership of these seals, which were highly valued for their fur. Canadian sealers countered that they could freely exploit the resource, as the seals were caught in international waters. Japanese schooners also frequented the area and took seals. While Canadians and Americans plied their trade, seal populations plummeted from an estimated 2.5 million in 1867 to approximately 400,000 by 1898. This represented a loss of income to sealers and a loss of revenue to the American government. Also, the public came to regard the harvest of the adorable seals as barbaric treatment. The mammals' cuteness struck a chord with the North American public. The public's fondness was fuelled by artist Henry Wood Elliot's illustrations. Hailing from Cleveland, Ohio, Elliot first arrived on the islands in 1872 and became enamoured of the setting, and especially the seals. He conducted semi-scientific surveys of the mammals, and his *The Seal-islands of Alaska* (1876), replete with illustrations (including one that showed them being bludgeoned to death), informed readers of the seals' plight. This was the era of the realistic animal story, and the public had come to sympathize with 'the kindred of the wild' (to borrow the phrase of Charles G.D. Roberts). Scientific arguments against the trade in seal furs also informed the debate, as David Starr Jordan and other American scientists demonstrated that female seals were taken faster than the herds could naturally replace them, thus signalling that a species collapse was eminent. Thus, after twenty-five years of wrangling over the issue, the North Pacific Fur Seal Convention of 1911 imposed a seven-year moratorium on the killing of seals. Canada was also financially compensated by the US for its loss of income during this period.

The centrepiece of the early Canadian/American agreements was the Migratory Birds Convention of 1916 (later the Migratory Bird Treaty of 1918). A multitude of winged species faced threats from market hunters in the plumage (millinery) trade, farmers who saw birds as nuisances that ate crops, and shrinking wetland and forest habitats. In 1905 at his Kingsville, Ontario, sanctuary, Jack Miner had created a sort of refuge for thousands of birds that annually passed over his property. Yet, this was an isolated case. The rise of the Audubon Society and citizen groups (often consisting of female majorities) protested the indiscriminate killing of birds on scientific and moral or sentimental grounds. In this context, Dr C. Gordon Hewitt of the Dominion Department of Agriculture emerged as a major voice in the debates surrounding the drafting of international policy. In his own field, entomology, he believed birds were underutilized in insect control, and as a result, Hewitt became a strong proponent and public advocate of the proposed treaty. The Migratory Bird Treaty imposed closed seasons and restrictions on the transport and sale of birds, and provided for the appointment of game officers to enforce the provisions; moreover, it enumerated which species were off limits to hunters.

Air pollution was addressed between the mid-1920s and 1941. The Pacific Northwest was the stage for one of the most significant environmental law cases of the twentieth century. The smelting and refining of base metals were important to the economy and the mobilization effort during World War I, and the railroads on both sides of the border ensured a high degree of commerce until the post-war recession. Consolidated Mining and Smelter Company of Canada (a subsidiary of the CPR) had a lead and zinc smelter in Trail, British Columbia, near the Washington State border. The company also produced chemical fertilizers. In 1921, a lead smelter at Northport, Washington, closed, leaving three hundred Americans without work. The Great Depression sunk the region into dire straits, and the success of the Canadian smelter did not help to secure cross-border goodwill. Farmers in Stevens County, Washington, were perplexed at the low yield of their crops. When they pondered the source of their problems, their eyes wandered across the border to the Trail smelter. The Montreal firm responsible for the emissions compensated the farmers after the first round of complaints. But the amount was not enough, and the aggrieved farmers formed the Citizens' Protective Association and demanded more in damages. Citizens demonstrated an obvious connection to the land that had provided livelihoods. Although farmers practiced small-scale agriculture amidst industrial activities (i.e., the timber camps and the copper smelter on the American side) they drew the line at the Trail smelter's harmful emissions and fought the company in and out of court for twenty years. After the first complaints, the Trail company installed state-of-the-art fume control technologies that lowered the daily tonnage of emission. The issue persisted beyond the local level when, in 1927, the IJC was brought in to investigate the matter. In 1931, the IJC decided that $350,000 should be awarded to the farmers, but it was far less than they had hoped. They continued their fight. By 1941, the matter came to a conclusion, and produced the precedent-setting 'polluter pays' principle that is still applied in such cases where emissions drift far from their source, even over international boundaries. The Trail smelter case in the first half of the twentieth century brought to light an important element of the current debate on climate change: pollution produced at one site has wide-ranging effects on far-off locales.

The continental commons could also encompass what many consider to be a uniquely Canadian river: the St Lawrence. In the 1950s, when Canadian and American governments wished to modify the river, few considered the venture to be a grand departure from the past. After all, the Lachine Canal's construction had tamed the rough rapids south of Montreal as early as 1825. St Lawrence Seaway and Power Project forever changed the lives of those on both sides of the great international river. The project meant dredging the river to enable deep-draft container ships to pass through to Lake Ontario, and harnessing current at Massena, New York, and near Cornwall, Ontario, for energy production. Unfortunately achieving these goals meant that residents in the path of construction had to be relocated. On the Canadian side, for example, twenty thousand acres were flooded on land belonging to sixty-five hundred people and including over 450 farms. Homeowners were offered market value for their property (which had been declining for years since initial plans for the project were made known) or compensation for their houses to be physically moved to another location. Some viewed the chance to move to new locations with optimism, while others felt bitter that their way of life was being put asunder against their wishes. Summer cottagers were not pleased to give up their places of refuge. Grave sites and historical landmarks were also moved. The local economy that had sprung up around angling, especially for muskellunge, yellow pickerel, and sturgeon, also suffered as the riverine ecology was altered. Like the shoreline residents, some fish were trapped by the thousands and relocated to other sites along the river as the natural course of the St Lawrence was diverted during construction of the power dam. Waters muddied from dredging were hardly desirable spots for anglers until well after the project was complete. The clearing of trees, shrubs, and other vegetation also led to bird depopulation. On the Canadian side, gas stations were removed, but the underground storage tanks were not; as a result, the water quality declined markedly to the extent that local users could not drink from the river as they once did. One resident looked back angrily, stating, 'I'd like people to realize how beautiful the river was with all the islands and rapids . . . I've told my kids about it. We lost so much beauty when we lost the rapids. I loved growing up near the river; I liked it the way it was' (Cox et al. 251). As we have seen in numerous examples from this chapter, conservation measures and multiple-use development came most often at the expense of local residents.

Conclusion

Progressively, resources came to be regarded as crucial to the daily lives of Canadians at the local, national, and continental levels. The state's crafting of resource policy and correct and incorrect uses of resources indicate that it was playing an ever-increasing role in the shaping of environmental discourse, and, in turn, social policy. The continental nature of the North American commons also made it paramount that the state play the lead role vis-à-vis its American neighbour in coordinating policies that would protect aquatic species, birds, and the air. This trend toward regulation and management of nature caused common people to become more and more distanced from that natural world. This is not to imply that other visions of nature did not exist during this period, however. An equally potent impulse was present, that of romanticism and the belief that the preservation of nature for its own sake was as important as economic reasons for conserving resources. It is this idea of the preservation of nature that we take up in the next chapter.

3

Romanticism and the Preservation of Nature (1800s and 1900s)

If utilitarian conservation sought the efficient management of resources for future use, then romantic preservation embraced the emotional connection that humans share with nature. Both impulses coexisted in Canada from the beginnings of sustained settlement into the early twentieth century. Nature became relegated to islands of oasis in a sea of increasing industrialization, urbanization, and immigration; an idea whose genesis can be found in French philosophe Jean-Jacques Rousseau's writings about the individual and society and the poetry of William Wordsworth, among others. Overall, the early nineteenth century saw a glorification of the sublime and the picturesque.

Both founding European groups coveted nature. Some sought in the wilds a reinvigoration of their Anglo-Saxon heritage through the celebration of nature, viewing the land as an inspiration and a national symbol. Landscape painters were especially prominent in this regard, and promoted a natural and pure image of Canada. This impulse also swept up interest among parks supporters and outdoor recreationists who regarded the protection of wild spaces as a high civic duty. In French Canada, *le roman de la terre* (the novel of the land) prized the land as one of the pillars (alongside language and Catholicism) that served as bulwarks against English-language domination and foreign (English-Canadian and American) procurement of natural resources.

As cities increasingly became the place of residence for Canadians, 'nature' or 'wilderness' began to represent a refuge from the often chaotic pace of life in an overcrowded, dirty metropolis. Social-class standing also informed the intellectual climate. Indeed, those fearing a dissipation of vital energy during this frenetic age heaped praise on the benefits of what was believed to be pristine wilderness and the many chances for revitalization it held for a bourgeoisie seeking respite and solace. Natural scenes could also strengthen historic links. The origins of tourism in Ontario, discussed below, serve as an illustration of how the variables of regeneration and remembrance coalesced during the first half of the nineteenth century.

Tourists – members of the upper to middle classes with leisure time to travel – differed in important ways from the settled residents of the lands they visited. While settlers struggled to support themselves on the land, physically shaping it in ways that fit their needs, tourists traversed landscapes in search of the next source of splendour. Moreover, such visitors brought with them a romantic-era vocabulary that they drew upon when judging or categorizing the places they viewed. The 'sublime' conjured images of gloom; irregularity of landscape, jagged rocks, sweeping hills and mountains, or the bewilderment of the dense, dark, menacing forests that struck early travellers. For many visitors to Canada, Niagara Falls was the embodiment of all that was sublime. The 'picturesque,' on the other hand, denoted a more soothing, less emotion-provoking vision that might be found at the scene of a family homestead; such pastoral landscapes harkened tourists back to a simpler, pre-industrial period characterized by a slower pace of life. The Muskoka region became a mainstay in this category. The words 'primitive' and 'savage' could also be employed to separate tourists from the worlds they encountered. Use of such symbolic language courses through nineteenth-century Euro-Canadian and American travellers' descriptions of lands marginally inhabited by Aboriginals, such as St Regis (Akwesasne) or the Garden Reserve near Sault Ste Marie.

A rough sort of parlance emerged around the 'civilized' meeting the 'uncivilized.'

Niagara Falls occupied the pages of nearly every tourist guide written about North America during the nineteenth century. Indeed, it might well be regarded as the pre-eminent tourist destination on the continent; perhaps because of the magnitude of falling water and its link with human sensibilities. The thundering, near-volcanic crashing of water to the depths of the basin produced in onlookers chills that few other experiences could match. Niagara Falls brought forth primordial emotions, setting the standard against which other tourist sites were judged. As word of the falls' natural features spread in Europe and North America, and after American access was facilitated with the 1825 completion of the Erie Canal, the spot became adorned with other historic symbols that recalled similarly blood-curdling sensations. Following the War of 1812, local residents kept the memory of the clash between American invaders and Upper Canadian defenders alive and used this to create a regional tourist trade. The joining of battlefield heroics with the natural grandeur of the falls hastened the sense of the sublime, and fused it with a presentation of recent human history at the ruins of Fort Erie; the battlefields of Chippewa, Lundy's Lane, and Queenston Heights (where one could also find a monument to General Sir Isaac Brock, fallen hero of the campaign); and the outpost at Fort George. Tourists marvelled at how the landscape came alive as it also preserved history.

Nature and Canadian Imperialism

Attitudes about the environment and its ability to influence human behaviour and temperament were ripe in Victorian-era English Canada, especially among those intellectuals espousing sympathies toward the Canada First movement. Intensely pro-British, sometimes of Loyalist origin, and seeing Canada's future as wedded to the time-tested strength of the British Empire, the Canada First movement sought a theory of Anglo-Saxon racial superiority rooted in the cold climes of Canada. The Imperial Federation League, the British Empire League in Canada, and especially the United Empire Loyalists members posited that having descended from northern peoples such as the Anglo-Saxons, Vikings, Teutons, Celts, and Norman French, Canadians should certainly take a leadership role in the world. Spokesmen included poet Charles Mair, Colonel George Taylor Denison, Queen's University principal George Monro Grant, writer and McGill University political economy professor Stephen Leacock, Upper Canada College principal Sir George R. Parkin, and especially Robert Grant Haliburton. They all celebrated the imperial tie to Great Britain and wished to distinguish Canada as a North American nation.

Social Darwinism also informed this group's views of culture and nature. Haliburton proffered that because northern peoples were dominant in Europe, they should also be dominant in North America. In all, the cold temperatures had moulded and would preserve free, strong, intelligent, industrious peoples with strong ties across the Atlantic to the Old World and its supposedly superior customs. Gender entered into the portrait as well, as it was surmised that 'northern' and 'cold' were male qualities, whereas females were 'southern' and 'warm.' Though perhaps not fully accepting the racial overtones of this view, the Group of Seven reinforced the image of the North as wedded to 'Canadianness' through their paintings in the early twentieth century. This portrait shaped the way Canadians saw themselves, as well as how the outside world saw Canada.

Le roman de la terre

The French-Canadian response to the English-Canadian embrace of imperialism was the intensely place-based *le roman de la terre* perspective. The message of this genre can be encapsulated in many possible examples, including the two works of literature discussed here. The first was written by a Frenchman, Louis Hémon. His *Maria Chapdelaine* (1914) tells of attachment, identity, and perseverance. The story's sixteen-year-old heroine must choose one of three suitors: François Paradis, Lorenzo Surprenant, and Eutrope Gagnon. François, her true love, dies while returning home through a blizzard. Lorenzo has returned from the factory scene of industrial New England to settle his family's estate; he is openly critical of the agricultural life that Maria's family pursues (at one point he charges that the farmers are 'slaves to [their] animals') (Hémon 133). Lorenzo tempts Maria with tales of the good life in the modern, albeit English-language dominated, United States. Eutrope finally wins her hand. He is a steady, determined farmer of the hardscrabble Saguenay land near the Peribonka River. When Maria's mother dies (after a life of hard work in remote settlements), she must make the choice: stay and duplicate her mother's traditional life; or, leave her home for the possibility of an easier time in America. One night, before deciding, she is visited by the 'voices' of Quebec's past. The first voice recalls the nature of the seasons, from the harshness of winter to the rebirth and glory of spring and summer. Another voice speaks of the founding of the land by French settlers from an ocean away, those who left their footprint and language on old Quebec. Lastly, the strongest message reaches her ears. It is a blend of a woman's singing and a priest sermonizing, 'the voice of the land of Québec' (ibid. 184). It reminds her,

We came here three hundred years ago, and we stayed . . . We have set our mark on a great piece of the new continent, from Gaspé to Montréal, from Saint-Jean d'Iberville to Ungava, saying: Here, all the things we brought with us, our religion, our language, our virtues and even our weaknesses, become sacred and intangible things that must endure to the end. All around us strangers have come, we like to call them barbarians. They have taken most of the power and most of the money; but in this land of Québec nothing has changed . . . And we have survived, perhaps so that in several centuries the world may turn toward us and say: These people belong to a race that does not know how to die . . . In Québec nothing must die, nothing must change. (ibid. 184–5)

After much soul searching, Maria stays in Quebec.

Another example of an important *le roman de la terre* is Félix-Antoine Savard's 1937 work, *Menaud, maître-draveur* (*Master of the River*). The story is set during the 1920s and 1930s in Mainsal, in the Charlevoix region of Quebec, and tells the tale of sixty-year-old master log driver Menaud and his struggle to save his mountain and the forests that shroud it from outsiders. It is unclear whether the outsiders are English-Canadians or Americans, though given the US direct investment in Canada, and especially Quebec, during the period in which Savard put pen to paper, we might surmise that it is the latter group. The subtext intimates a French-Canadian defence of its land and heritage against those who would lease, develop, and otherwise claim the terrain upon which Menaud's people had trod for more than three hundred years. Savard's story, borrowing from the character of Lorenzo Surprenant in Hémon's novel, also contains a turncoat/collaborator/opportunist: Delie (the wolverine). Delie seeks to ingratiate himself to the foreigners, and also to take the hand of the master driver's only daughter, Maria. By the novel's end, Menaud becomes mad in his quest to protect the mountain forests that teem with life: '[t]his natural world had seemed to love him from that now distant day when he [at age ten] had committed himself to its knowledge. It gave him the pure and unsullied mountain air . . . water . . . wood . . . fish of its lakes too, the game of its thickets . . . ' (Savard 44). In the end, however, the rebellion of one man against outsiders was not enough to halt the speed of progress.

The wedding of land and tradition was a mainstay of such novels, demonstrating the centrality of place in the changing world of industrialization, and the luring of young people away from Quebec between the 1830s and 1930s, when it is estimated that about one million people left their home province to pursue livelihoods in the United States.

Creating a New Canadian Aesthetic

Two sorts of landscape paintings emerged during the nineteenth and early twentieth centuries that demonstrated an attachment to place. In the first variety, idealized representations, artistic licence was key. The artist portrayed the landscape – often a pastoral setting – to fit with the romantic image in his or her mind's eye, rather than as it actually existed. The second variety of landscape paintings effected a commodification of the land, displaying a landscape that could be used either to promote tourism or to secure a sense of Canadian identity that was linked to nature.

The first type was particularly present in Lower Canada following the Conquest of 1760, when the colony was handed from French to British hands. British topographic renderings (drawn by military surveyors and meant for the eyes of kings, ministers, aristocrats, and politicians) most often showcased a tranquil, picturesque, and ideal landscape. As if to suggest that the stage was set for an image makeover, such 'colonial landscapes' presumed that as the British Empire took shape, the human costs of building a global empire – the suppression of Scottish clans, the assimilation of French-Canadian *habitants*, the uneasy peace between Aboriginal peoples and Anglo-American colonists in trans-Appalachian America, and Caribbean slavery – could be erased from the portrait that was emerging in the minds of Britons. By presenting panoramic vistas, military artists introduced the idea that the land was ripe for the transplantation of British culture and progressive designs.

In the early twentieth century, the Group of Seven likewise erased the Aboriginal presence when depicting the northern landscapes that they found so fascinating. Tom

Thomson's *The Jack Pine* (1916) and *The West Wind* (1917), along with Frederick Varley's *Stormy Weather, Georgian Bay* (1921), presented the landscape as devoid of humans and animals, recreating it as 'wild.' It is curious that these artists purposely erased wildlife and Aboriginal peoples from the landscape, since other writers and travellers celebrated them as essential parts of the 'wilderness experience.' Emily Carr, a contemporary of the Group of Seven who was mentored and heavily influenced by member Lawren Harris, is famous for her representations of West Coast Aboriginal groups. She painted totem poles into her scenes to evince the past and present inhabitation of the land by Aboriginal peoples, thus acknowledging not only their presence but also their possession of the land. The Group of Seven, rather than depicting humans in their paintings, anthropomorphized the natural landscape to represent an image they held about Canadian people. In Thomson's famous *Jack Pine,* the tree takes on a human quality. A lone pine perched at the water's edge, having braced for years against the ravages of a harsh, unrelenting wind, symbolizes the essential Canadian spirit, characterized by a resistance to the often-harsh climate of the North and a will to soldier on.

The commodification of the Canadian landscape through painting has also been a technique of artists since the nineteenth century. William Henry Bartlett's renditions of Upper and Lower Canada are prime examples. The English painter visited the Canadas in 1838, a few years after completing a series of sketches of the United States. Bartlett sought to impose picturesque and sublime imagery on the land. In many ways, his desire to eliminate humans and their activities (such as forest clearance, farming, and canal and road building) from his interpretations was a nod to the use of romantic codes to present Canada to Europeans, if not to Canadians themselves. He sketched forest scenes that played up the Aboriginal presence, likened the lakes of Lower Canada to those of the Alps region, and painted church spires emanating from the villages along the St Lawrence River that recalled the solemnity of New France. Similarly, scenes from the Bay of Quinte presented fishers hauling nets to shore (an activity that hardly hinted at the rising industrial age) and shepherds tending their flocks amidst prosaic village scenes. Bartlett was also enamoured of Niagara Falls. In his sketches of this natural wonder, the sublime reigns supreme as miniscule human figures clutch at the rocks while struggling to glimpse the enormity of the falls in all its roaring glory.

Between 1882 and 1884, the tour de force in Canadian tourist literature appeared in two volumes: *Picturesque Canada: The Country as It Was and Is*, by George Monro Grant. Much of the art that accompanied the essays was provided by Lucius O'Brien, who had made a name for himself with his 1880 painting *Sunrise on the Saguenay*. O'Brien later went on to paint scenes of the Northwest to promote the CPR. Other volumes of Canadian tourist literature followed *Picturesque Canada*, such as those by Charles G.D. Roberts and William Wilfred Campbell, who brought their own creative energies to bear in aggrandizing their country. They delivered the message that tourists would become enveloped in the picturesque and awed by the sublime vistas of Canada. Indeed, Campbell (in this somewhat exaggerated example) saw the natural landscape as protecting a burgeoning identity on the northern half of the continent. He wrote that the four Great Lakes bordering Ontario had shielded the province from the United States and the Northwest 'so that the Canadian soil, the Canadian seasons, and the Canadian atmosphere, have been allowed to produce a peculiar stock of a British American people, which is already taking its place as a national factor among the ethical forces and race elements of the world' (Bentley 58). For those espousing such an imperialist viewpoint, the natural qualities of British North America had served to forge a unique, sturdy, 'northern race.'

Arguably, the Group of Seven and Emily Carr have provided the most lasting and omnipresent images of Canada's natural environment. Since the 1920s these artists' visual interpretations of the Canadian landscape have left an imprint on the minds of those living within and outside of Canada. They celebrated a 'northern distinctness.' Lawren Harris believed in the painter's unique ability to transmit to the Canadian public a sense of belonging to a place that sits perched at

the top of the continent [and remains a] source of spiritual flow that will ever shed clarity into the growing race of America, and we Canadians being closest to this source seem destined to produce an art somewhere different from our southern fellows – an art more spacious, of a greater living quiet, perhaps of a more certain conviction of eternal values. We were not placed between the Southern teeming of men and the ample replenishing North for nothing. (Osborne 172)

Provincial and National Parks

Where better to capture and witness nature's grandeur than in the pristine (or what were thought to be pristine) settings of parks? The political economy of parks (and park making) is a story grounded in the government desire to reserve tracts of (usually forested) land so as to ensure that future supplies of timber resources were available to future generations. By setting aside forested land for the purposes of both business and recreation, park making was the very essence of 'utilitarian conservation' thinking. Yet, romantic preservationist sentiments also influenced debates on parks and their value to the public.

In 1887, Queen Victoria Niagara Falls became the first provincial park in Canada, a creation of the Ontario government. The province and business interests saw a chance to both promote the history of the region (a key battleground in the War of 1812) and attract tourists. Ontario continued to set aside more sites to accommodate the aims of preservationists as well as the desires of recreationists for outdoor activities, and provincial parks at Algonquin (1893), Rondeau (1894), Burlington Beach (1907), Quetico (1913), Long Point (1921), Presqu'ile (1922), Ipperwash (1938), Sibley (1944), and Lake Superior (1944) emerged in succession. For similar reasons – preserving forests and wild lands, promoting recreation, and celebrating heritage – Quebec also set aside spaces for public parks. Between 1895 and 1938, the province created le Parc des Laurentides, le Parc de la Montagne Tremblante, le Parc de la Gaspésie, and le Parc du Mont Orford. Three of these parks were established close to the province's largest city, Montreal, so as to be easily accessible to city dwellers and tourists alike.

The federal government began creating parks around the same time. The Rocky Mountains Park Act of 1887 paved the way for the creation of a larger system of parks. This act set aside Banff Springs, which had demonstrated therapeutic qualities for those with respiratory maladies. By placing Banff beyond the reach of developers, Sir John A. Macdonald declared as prime minister that such places were to 'be brought at once into usefulness' (Brown 49). The advent of the park at Banff, with its CPR link and its improvement through the construction of roads, bridges, and other amenities (such as hotels), would assist in popularizing the region that heretofore had not been successful in luring large numbers of settlers or tourists. The move served to showcase the healthful possibilities of the region, and to do for the Canadian Rockies what Hot Springs, Arkansas, had done for tourism in the post-Reconstruction US South, or what the Trudeau Institute at Saranac Lake, New York, had done for Adirondack vacationing. The passage of the Dominion Parks Act (1911) and its further protection of scenic areas entrenched the parks idea.

Recreationists applauded the Parks Branch policy of bringing federal power to bear on questions of protecting the inviolability of public space. The Bow River's development at the start of the twentieth century offers an example of how parks administrators and outdoor enthusiasts joined forces to block what they regarded as the ruination of (public) landscapes by developers. The Alpine Club of Canada (ACC) was one of the most prominent recreational groups of the day. Avid climbers, its members coveted the vistas of the Rockies. Not only did they defend their right to access the parks; they also waged a battle to protect designated areas from hydroelectric development.

The ACC was a nationwide organization dedicated to the promotion of mountaineering and the celebration of Canada's mountain heritage. The club favoured the opening of the mountains as national playgrounds and wished also to preserve wildlife, plants, habitats, and striking scenes. Surveyor Arthur Oliver Wheeler and journalist Elizabeth Parker founded the club in 1906; by 1922 the organization claimed 599 members, mostly from the urban, English-speaking bourgeoisie of Canada, the United States, and Great Britain. Following World War I, James B. Harkin assumed the role of Dominion Parks Commissioner; he favoured widening the circle of the flora and fauna to be guarded inside the parks. By the 1920s the ACC and Harkin reinforced one another's missions.

Challenges to the inviolability of parks soon emerged. The post-World War I era in Alberta saw the increasing need for water to irrigate southern prairie farms and to furnish electricity to burgeoning cities like Calgary and Lethbridge. Drought gripped the region and business leaders and farmers clamoured for assistance. The proposal to build a dam in Waterton Lakes National Park quickly mobilized the ACC and Harkin. According to the federal government's plan, water would be stored behind a dam and fed through irrigation canals to needy farms. The dam was to be developed by the CPR and its local subsidiary, the Alberta Railway and Irrigation Company. From the start, Harkin opposed the idea, arguing that the use of resources from within the park's boundaries ran contrary to the original aims of the parks notion; that is, to protect and maintain the pristine natural landscape and the resources contained therein. Moreover, he enunciated his belief in the inviolability of parks, which he asserted 'are the property of all the people of Canada . . . they should not be developed for the benefit of any one section of the country or for private interests' (Reichwein 132). Wheeler offered Harkin the assistance of the ACC, and by 1923 sounded the clarion call: '[H]ands off our national parks' (Armstrong et al. 133). Steadfast opposition by both Commissioner Harkin and the ACC stifled the project proposal, and it died by 1923. However, with the onset of the Second World War and the need for more energy during wartime, the quest to power Calgary with current from the Bow River became a reality.

Following the Second World War, public interest in parks and recreation once again spiked. Ontarians in particular flocked to provincial parks. The province felt the baby boom in a significant way: its population rose from 3.8 million in 1946 to 6.2 million in 1961. Most Ontarians lived in the province's south-central region, in the concentrated urban areas where industrialization prevailed. The Great Depression and Second World War had forced people to save or wisely spend the little money they had. As well-paying jobs returned in the 1940s, Ontarians finally had more disposable income and leisure time, and many people bought cars. All these variables pushed people outdoors, especially to spend more time with their children. Record numbers of visitors ventured to campgrounds and parks like Lake of Two Rivers, Algonquin, Ipperwash, Rondeau, and others. Between 1954 and 1967 a new impetus was placed upon acquiring lands in both northern and southern Ontario. A more egalitarian mood prevailed, which sought to include not only wealthy cottagers, but visitors of modest means as well. A new, more open and accessible park act was announced in December 1954 by Premier Leslie Frost. An explosion of new park openings followed, and the province went from eight parks in 1954 to seventy-seven in 1961. Moreover, a nearly 300 per cent increase in parks attendance occurred between 1957 (approximately 2.1 million visitors) and 1961 (an estimated 6.2 million visitors). A staggering 261 provincial parks would be under the supervision of the province by 1989.

Science and preconceptions about what should be included in parks also played a role in the park-making story. Canada's western national parks provide perspective on the state of human/nature relations, specifically those that centred upon bison and wolves. The North American bison was of importance to both the sustenance and culture of Aboriginal peoples. Yet, as Euro-Canadian permanent settlement extended west, this valued resource was put in jeopardy. In the United States the slaughter of bison herds was intentional, a deliberate means of starving resistant Aboriginal groups into submission. In Canada, the decline of the bison was linked to an overexploitative trade in tanned buffalo robes, and it took only eighty years (from the beginning of the nineteenth century to 1880) for the animals to disappear from the Canadian Prairies.

Yet, the bison were arguably *the* symbol of the West – or at least the imagined West that tourists desired to see when they travelled to places such as the Banff Springs Hotel. Such scenic trappings of the region were essential to the longevity of the tourist industry in the West, so it became necessary for reasons of commerce to protect the bison and other species. In 1911, wood bison from the United States were transplanted to Alberta. Their arrival was intended for the establishment of Buffalo National Park near Wainwright, which began as the idea of Michel Pablo, a private citizen with a herd of bison but no land on which to graze them. At Canadian government expense, the 703 head of plains bison was purchased and relocated to Alberta. This sort of enterprise led to the establishment of other western national parks: Glacier/Yoho (1886), Waterton Lakes (a forest reserve, 1895), Jasper (1907), and Buffalo (1908). The reintroduction of the bison into the parks also led to rising numbers of visitors: in 1887 there were three thousand visitors; by 1912, the number had risen to over seventy-three thousand.

While bison seemed to be the most glorified of the western species, a throwback to the times when Aboriginal peoples hunted on foot and horseback, wolves symbolized the savage nature of the West that might turn visitors away. To that end, Parks Commissioner Harkin encouraged members of his department to hunt wolves and coyotes. Wolves were seen as predators and a grave threat to the idealistic vision that Harkin and others had for the parks, wherein visitors could experience a sort of controlled nature without worrying about such menacing creatures. Park wardens did the dirty work, often maintaining trap lines that accidentally killed marten, mink, and other fur-bearing animals whose fur was more valuable than the wolf's. Some members of the general public objected to the practice of killing wolves, and scientific wisdom about the necessity of natural predators was also contrary to the prevailing policy. Nonetheless, the killing of wolves continued until at least the 1940s.

Similar steps to fashion parks according to pre-existing social and cultural attitudes appeared in Atlantic Canada. Although outwardly a positive step toward celebrating the natural heritage of the region, the establishment of four new parks by the National Parks Branch (Cape Breton Highlands in 1936, Prince Edward Island in 1936, Fundy in 1947, and Terra Nova in 1957) did not come without controversy. At Cape Breton Highlands, some species of fauna, including beaver, moose, and Atlantic salmon, had to be either reintroduced or artificially stocked, while at Prince Edward Island trout were planted in the hope of adding to the maritime characteristics of the region. In order to combat the spruce budworm outbreaks of the 1950s, a similar interventionist policy was pursued and the pesticide DDT was used to prevent the spread of the insect. Thus, newer parks became proving grounds for the emerging science of ecology, but in ways that seemed to run contrary to the idea of preserving natural lands in their untamed state. Such cases serve to demonstrate that even the supposedly enlightened prophets of the new science came to the situation with their own preconceptions of how wild a place should be.

Conclusion

Romantic preservation was manifested in many ways. It stimulated the nationalist psyches of English and French speakers, and for the former, it buoyed the message of Canadian imperialism with images of hearty, stalwart, northerners. Painters and park enthusiasts were inspired. The former influenced Canadians' perceptions of a nature tied to national identity, while the latter influenced park managers' ideas about what nature should encompass and what should be found in Canadian parks. Contact with forests and wild animals could soothe the tensions that arose from urban life in Canada. And, back to earlier prompts, Canada's wilds could rejuvenate the physical and emotional ties that the imperialist-minded English Canadian, the 'Northman of the New World,' possessed (Kaufmann 682). Likewise, Francophone novelists of the *le roman de la terre* genre, who located Quebec's identity at least in part through an attachment to place, pursued a romantic point of view. As the next chapter reveals, the Arcadian point of view and the national attachment that both English and French speakers attributed to their land pulsed as much after the Second World War as before. As industrial activity transformed and polluted many landscapes in the second half of the twentieth century, some Canadians saw a renewed connection with nature (often for its own sake) as necessary if the human species – and perhaps the country – were to survive. The concept of environmentalism, or caring for the land as proactive human stewards, continues to course through contemporary debates about the treatment of the natural world – not only in Canada, but globally. In the period from the 1950s to the 2000s, an environmental movement (first confined to local issues, but later embracing more global concerns) took shape and has come to characterize Canada in a way that the conservation versus preservation debate did for earlier generations.

4

Environmentalism (1950s to 2000s)

For Western capitalist nations such as Canada, the post-Second World War era ushered in a new period of economic growth. The economy expanded and yielded a rate of growth in real gross national product of 5.1 per cent between 1950 and 1973. Growth was especially pronounced in heavy industry and traditional staples like forestry. Young people, having emerged from the twin crises of their age – economic dislocation and war – finally felt positive that better times lay ahead. This renewed confidence inspired them to marry early and reproduce at a noteworthy pace between 1946 and 1965, in what demographers call the baby boom. During this period, the national population went from 12.3 million to 19.6 million, and the number of annual births rose from 343,504 to 419,000. Larger families created a need for more and larger living spaces, which led to the augmentation of large cities like Toronto and the creation of the suburbs. Once members of the baby boom generation became of university age, they entered an expanded higher education system in just about every province, and began to frame their own ideas about their place in the world, both human and natural.

In the second half of the twentieth century, Canada was in a phase of prosperity and expansion that unfortunately contributed to environmental degradation. Increasing consumer needs and demands conspired to set a mood where science was employed in the task of coaxing more and more from the environment through dramatic modifications to local environments, the introduction of new chemicals for a wide range of uses, and the overharvesting of wildlife.

At the same time, a new way of conceiving of the natural environment was also on the rise since the 1960s. It came in direct response to previous generations' misuse of the environment. To say that youth were fully credited with this reversal of opinion would be a gross exaggeration, since there were critical voices who were born before the Great Depression and had an enormous impact on this new trend (such as American Rachel Carson, author of *Silent Spring*). However, the force of the baby boom generation, with its own set of concerns for a better treatment of their world, had much to do with the turnabout. In the realm of science, ecology was gaining more and more acceptance as an omnibus way to conceive of the natural world; in essence, it was a marshalling of the life sciences into one concerted analysis to explain how species functioned, not individually, but in the larger world (or ecosystem).

The 1960s to the 1990s was also a period when well-publicized, human-created environmental catastrophes spurred action and forced Canadians and others to question the way they lived. The global environmental movement might well have begun with the 1962 publication of Carson's *Silent Spring*, and its ominous message that widespread and reckless use of pesticides such as DDT could reach and potentially harm humankind. Around the same time, mercury poisoning affected the health of fishers and citizens in Minamata, Japan. The 1967 *Torrey Canyon* oil spill in the North Sea and the 1969 Santa Barbara, California, spill focused attention on the world economy's dependence on petroleum. In an apocalyptic scene, the Cuyahoga River in Ohio, which had long been treated as a dumping ground for chemical companies, caught fire in 1969. A near melt-down at the Three Mile Island nuclear station near Harrisburg, Pennsylvania, in 1979 prompted many to question the wisdom of such facilities. Love Canal, New York, was a residential community that was built upon a toxic waste dump. Around 1978, the community received global attention because citizens were falling ill with various cancers and other life-threatening sicknesses. An even deadlier situation arose at the Union Carbide plant in Bhopal, India, in 1984, when three thousand people perished after fatal gas leaked from the plant. The Chernobyl, Ukraine, nuclear station disaster in April 1986 devastated a generation and wafted atomic particles over much of Northern Europe. Popular culture reflected the changing mood: musician Joni Mitchell's 'Big Yellow Taxi' (1970) lamented overindustrialization, the spread of chemicals, and general urban blight, and Gordon Lightfoot's 1977 hit song 'The Wreck of the Edmund Fitzgerald' spoke of a technology-laden age and humans who tempted fate by not respecting the power of nature, namely Lake Superior and its November gales. People seriously questioned whether the way they were conducting their lives was a threat to the planet's future.

Environmentalism in its North American sense may be best understood through the work of American historian Samuel P. Hays. He distils it to three elements: beauty (i.e., of green or wild spaces), health (i.e., public health), and permanence (i.e., society's demand after the Second World War to ensure the protection of the first two). We may broaden this definition by adding that the younger generation was questioning the wisdom of its parents' and grandparents' treatment of the environment. The young generation sought a more benign relationship with nature that limited pollution, created green spaces, and protected wildlife for its own sake. Ecology emphasized the interrelatedness of species and how events in one group could affect another, which was part of the holistic approach. In sum, environmentalism was about re-evaluating humanity's place amongst other living things in the world. Artistic expressions also hinted at a new relationship with nature. Citizen

action welled to push political agendas, again entrenching
the state in a multitude of nature-related affairs.

Critical Voices and Environmental Sustainability
in Canadian Arts and Letters

As we have seen in the writings of Catharine Parr Traill,
Ernest Thompson Seton, and Charles G.D. Roberts, popular writers would sometimes enter into environmental
debates. Like their historical counterparts, popular writers
of the mid-to-late twentieth century often brought environmental concerns to the national consciousness. Roderick
Haig-Brown was one of the first writer-spokesmen of the
post-Second World War era, a role he performed through
his adoption of British Columbia. The province brimmed
with the optimism of progress following the war, and politicians and businessmen were primed to exploit the resource
hinterland. Political leaders envisioned manifold industrial
development in mines, forests, hydroelectric dams, and
assorted mills, all of which consumed natural resources. As
Social Credit premier between 1952 and 1972, W.A.C. Ben-
nett was proud of these accomplishments. But Haig-Brown
questioned the wisdom of such development.

Haig-Brown was born in 1908 in Sussex, England, to a
privileged family. After receiving his education in England,
he sought adventure in the Pacific Northwest, and arrived
in the province during the 1920s. He worked as a log-
ger, trapper, and beachcomber, and later married and settled along the Campbell River. He served in the Second
World War and returned to Campbell River where, between
1941 and 1975, he was town magistrate. To most, however,
he became known through his books on angling during
the 1950s and 1960s, which sold well and were translated
into several languages. These books displayed his reverence for fair play and balance, stemming from the familiar
Waltonian impulse of generosity rather than competition

among anglers. Haig-Brown was also a conservationist, and gave public speeches on the subject. It was in this capacity that he waged an angry battle to stop the raising of the water level on his beloved Campbell River in 1951. Though Haig-Brown was only partially successful in defending the riverine environment against a hydroelectric project that was part of BC's economic boom, his reputation grew as a critic of industrial expansion that came at the expense of the environment. He also admonished the province's new forest policy, which allowed for large cuts of timber – even within the boundaries of provincial parks. Between 1948 and 1961 the province cut 1.9 million hectares out of a forest reserve that included 4.4 million hectares. Haig-Brown was acting as something of the rural gentleman/father-of-the-people type, and was strongly inspired by his childhood in the English countryside. Further, he regarded the protection of nature and the search for social equilibrium as part of his responsibilities as magistrate. He was not an opponent of capitalism or economic growth, but he did seek to temper those needs against environmental protection. In many ways, his omnibus 1961 definition of conservation guided his perspective:

it means having enough faith in the future and the needs of future people; it means accepting moral and practical restraints that limit self-interest . . . [it is also] a religious concept – the most universal and fundamental of all such concepts, the worship of fertility to which man has dedicated himself in every civilization since his race began. (Keeling 239)

With Haig-Brown's help, the human/nature discourse was wending its way into the regional, if not national, consciousness.

Writing from the natural history tradition, Fred Bodsworth offered a simple tale that roundly critiqued the harm that humans had done to migratory bird species. *Last of the Curlews* (1954) predated Carson's *Silent Spring* and laid a foundation for much of its argument. The story of the last male Eskimo curlew on earth is poignant and touching, lamenting the loss of his female mate(s) and foreshadowing the extinction of the species. The narrative borrows from the animal psychology model proffered by Seton, Roberts, and others of an earlier time. However, it also draws upon the known habits and migration routes of the curlews and other birds that annually travelled from the Arctic to Patagonia to breed and reproduce. Why had the species been reduced to only one, male, bird? The interspersed historical data tell the story: all along the migration path, from Labrador to South America, market hunters and sportsmen had decimated the flocks, beginning in the late nineteenth century. The nameless five-year-old curlew elicits sympathy from the reader. He instinctively follows the flight paths that have been imprinted upon his brain over generations, dodges predatory hawks, and negotiates the Gulf Stream winds and storms as he makes his way south to summering grounds, finally arriving eighty thousand miles later in Patagonia. At his destination he rests, and during the summer finally finds a female with which to mate. But, alas, as the two weave their way back to the Arctic, and the would-be nesting grounds, the female is shot and dies. The once-again solitary male is left to finish the journey homeward and begin his search for a mate anew. Bodsworth's narration presents the species with both manmade and natural dangers. However, the burden of blame is clearly placed upon the hunters for putting the Eskimo curlew on the same hopeless path to extinction as the ill-fated passenger pigeon.

Animals also captured the imagination of Farley Mowat in three texts he authored between 1963 and 1984. Mowat, however, approached his subject with a harder, more damning edge than Bodsworth. In *Never Cry Wolf* (1963), an instant bestseller, Mowat revived the realistic animal story of past generations. But the book raised the ire of wildlife biologists, who charged that Mowat told an incomplete story by not only exaggerating government scientists' treatment of the animal, but also being ignorant (or only half-informed) about wolves' natural habits. His book and the response to it recalled in important ways not only the 'nature faking' controversy that sprung up around depictions of animals in the work of Ernest Thompson Seton and Charles G.D. Roberts, but also the more recent reception to the Walt Disney film *Bambi* and the ensuing debate over hunting that it had sparked in the 1940s.

Seemingly straightforward, *Never Cry Wolf* is a partly biographical account of a young biologist who studies wolves on the Arctic tundra. However, a closer reading of the work reveals Mowat's wilderness advocacy, which, charged government scientists, cast the wolf not as a predator, but as a victim in the wild. The debate was heightened all the more due to Mowat's dubious scientific training, which had included a brief sojourn into biology.

The wolf has a long history in children's literature as a villain. In the case of Mowat and the Canadian tundra, wolves were considered predators that killed caribou. Yet, in an effort to rehabilitate the image of the animal, Mowat used *Never Cry Wolf* to introduce readers to George, Angeline, and other anthropomorphized characters whose animal qualities he selectively highlighted. Mowat disagreed with the Canadian Wildlife Service (CWS) scientists who regarded wolves as a menace, and brought personal observation and Aboriginal knowledge to the pages of his text. The fact that the story took place in the barren lands of the North only added to its exoticism, mysticism, and wonderment for many southern Canadians who had never visited the region. CWS spokesmen denounced Mowat, claiming that he took liberties with the data in order to weave a pleasurable yarn; they recalled from his brief career with the service that Mowat's nickname was 'Hardly Knowit' (Jones, '*Never Cry Wolf*' 75). Nonetheless, the novel sold over a million copies and was made into a movie by Walt Disney Pictures. By the mid-1960s, hundreds of visitors to Algonquin Provincial Park blocked roads so that they could participate in 'wolf howls.' Surely the book and its popularity produced a reassessment of the wolf, if not by scientists then by the reading public whose interest was piqued by this compelling plea to better understand the animal world. Mowat returned to similar themes of human arrogance in *A Whale for the Killing* (1972) and *Sea of Slaughter* (1984).

Best known as a novelist who celebrated a sort of pan-Canadianism, Hugh MacLennan also wrote the environment into history. He expressed a true concern for Canada's waterways in two collections of essays: *Seven Rivers of Canada* (1961) and *Rivers of Canada* (1974). The latter volume flowed as naturally from the first as the current of the St Lawrence River flowed past MacLennan's adopted home of Montreal. The 1961 version lauded the 'rivers that made a nation'; these were 'heroic' narratives that downplayed the European conquest of Aboriginal Canada and praised the spirit of explorers who filtered into the Northwest along natural aquatic highways. The 1974 version was quite different, however. The interim period of the contentious 1960s had seen the environmental movement take form and gain momentum. As a professor of English at McGill University, MacLennan was acutely aware of this change. *Rivers of Canada* was intended as a coffee-table book, replete with photographs of the rivers in question. Some of the original essays from 1961 were carried over, but in the newer river texts – for example those on the Humber, the Tobique and Mactaquac (tributaries of the St John), the Miramichi, the Albany, and the Thompson – real threats to the integrity of the waters, the fish that swam in them, and the people who lived along their banks loomed large. Reckless technology, damming, and poor public policy decisions had led, or were leading to, the ruin of these rivers, which 'define the character of the lands through which they flow' (Forkey 59). In all this 'progress,' humans were 'newcomers' that had elevated themselves above the need for pristine, healthy rivers; he urged his readers to '*think* like a river even though a river doesn't think. Because every river on this earth, some of them against incredible obstacles, ultimately finds its way through the labyrinth to the universal sea' (MacLennan, *Rivers of Canada* 8). Rivers, he continued, were

life-agents of incalculable importance . . . the life [source] of forest, grass, plants, fish, insects, birds, reptiles and animals . . . [they are the] arteries of their continents . . . think of major tributaries as the continent's veins . . . think of the uncountable number of small feeder streams as the capillaries of the earth. (Forkey 59)

His insistence upon seeing rivers within the corporeal whole of life inched MacLennan, like other writers, to express ideas about ecosystems and reverence for life; the fact that he linked these rivers to the greater Canadian experience only served to validate the characterization of him as a pan-Canadian writer.

Popular expression for defending the environment came in many different forms during the last half of the twentieth century. Purveyors of the written word in both English and French crafted discourses in which their protagonists became the stewards of the land, protectors against those that sought to possess the natural qualities that informed national identity. Two novelists in particular, Margaret Atwood and Jacques Godbout, used such currents to create iconographic characters that remain with us today.

An overt critique of the despoliation of Canada's wilderness is found in Margaret Atwood's *Surfacing* (1972). She weaves a tale fuelled by the search for individual pasts and the collective Canadian future. Four Toronto baby boomers travel to Northern Quebec in search of the father of the narrator, a nameless woman. The group encounter Americans who one paranoid character, David, believes will deal for Canada's vast supplies of fresh water: 'It's obvious,' he muses,

[t]hey're running out of water, clean water, they're dirtying up all of theirs, right? Which is what we have a lot of, this country is

almost all water . . . [in] ten years, they'll be up against the wall. They'll try to swing a deal with the [Canadian] government, get us to give them the water cheap or for nothing in exchange for more soapflakes or something, and the [Canadian] government will give in, they'll be a bunch of puppets as usual. (Atwood 97)

Commentary upon American foreign policy during the Vietnam War era and burgeoning feminism are additional subthemes spliced into this narrative that laments the loss of a pristine environment (including, for example, the utter stupidity of the human killing and desecration of a heron).

Jacques Godbout's *l'Isle au Dragon* (*Dragon Island*), a whimsical, fantastic retelling of the St George tale, also evinces an environmentalist undertone. In this novel, professional dragon slayer Michel Beauparlant squares off against the slimy, chauvinistic American developer William T. Shaheen. The story mirrors Savard's tale of the master log driver (described in chapter 3), though with a more immediate, neo-Marxist assault on US investment in Canada. The Texan, Shaheen, has leased Isle Verte in the St Lawrence River for thirty years. He has dispossessed its inhabitants and is readying the island for its new purpose: to become Quebec's first Controlled Atomic Dump (or CAD). The use of the acronym CAD, intimates the sellout nature of the Canadian government for sacrificing such treasured places only to allow, in protagonist Beauparlant's words, 'two hundred and thirty million [US] citizens [to defecate] in our direction! We've become America's garbagemen and the Saint Lawrence River is nothing anymore but an open sewer . . . ' (Godbout 66). Beauparlant even imagines the Anglicization of the island's name on American maps as Green Island. He therefore strikes out on a 'crusade to the holy land of ecology, in the hopes of promoting, fostering, and disseminating the mystical body that is clear air . . . ' (ibid. 42) so as to rid his home of this menace. In an interesting turn of events, the dragon slayer enlists the aid of a serpent in order to bring about the earthly demise of the foreigner, Shaheen. Atwood and Godbout sought not only to level criticisms at those who would despoil the earth, but also to threaten what purveyors of the counterculture believed to be the real menace: the economic liberalism that had reigned since the close of the Second World War. Journalists also took up this cause, as will be discussed in the example of the *Georgia Straight* below.

During this same period, Quebec artist and filmmaker Frédéric Back was creating graphic renditions of human excesses that were at the expense of the natural environment. He provided drawings, for example, to promote *le jour de la biosphère* (Earth Day) in 1971. Later, in film, he promoted the cause of reforestation in *L'homme qui plantait des arbres* (*The Man Who Planted Trees*, 1987), for which he won an Oscar. In *Le fleuve aux grandes eaux* (*The Mighty River*, 1993) he celebrated the St Lawrence River as a national symbol while decrying its pollution. More recently, through his artistic talent and activism, Back has supported various Quebec groups such as the *Société pour vaincre la pollution*, the S.O.S. Water Coalition, and *La Fondation Rivières*.

Environmental Activism

It is important to bear in mind the era in which this new environmentalism emerged. The sixties were ripe with calls for change of all sorts; and, if the progressive, Vancouver-based free weekly newspaper the *Georgia Straight* is any indication, the treatment of the natural world ranked prominently among these. In addition to advocating for women's and gay rights, abortion, the legalization of marijuana, and an end to nuclear weapons testing, the newspaper also weighed in on environmental issues. In February 1971, for example, the *Georgia Straight* editorialized against the proposed Cherry Point pipeline. The US oil pipeline project would transport hot oil from Alaska's North Slope to Valdez, where it would be loaded onto supertankers that would sail past the BC coast. If the pipeline was built above ground, it would block wildlife migration; but if it was buried below ground, it could be subject to buckling due to the surrounding permafrost. Moreover, water pollution would result from the refinery discharge or oil spills at the transport points. The newspaper based many of its claims against the project on well-publicized oil spills such as the ones at Santa Barbara in 1969 and San Francisco in January 1971, demonstrating the ongoing discourse on the environment and its protection that underlay the language of countercultural journalism. Critical views against pollution seemed to abound, and this climate of opinion helped to frame the establishment of two Canadian grassroots environmental groups, one radical (Greenpeace), the other more mainstream (Pollution Probe).

Greenpeace emerged as the most high-profile environmental activist group. The group's origins were embedded in the American New Left counterculture and popular ecology movements of the 1950s and 1960s. Rage over the United States' involvement in Southeast Asia, nuclear-weapons testing, and what members considered to be the rapacious commerce in whale products fuelled the drive of this group, which emerged in Vancouver in the late 1960s. In response to whaling, the Quaker tactic of 'bearing witness' (appearing at the scene of an activity and demonstrating disapproval), became a hallmark of Greenpeace. The famous photos of activists harassing steel-hulled whaling vessels from flimsy zodiac watercraft conjure up the most identifiable and romantic images of 'radical environmentalism.' As one early member, Rex Weyler, recalled, the group saw itself as part of a historical process, a product of the past as well as a contemporary answer to the new spirit of the age of ecology. 'Greenpeace represented an idea,' Weyler remembered, 'as well as an organization, an idea with a role to play at the interface between nature and society. Wish it or not, we had become Gaia's advocates, heirs to St Francis and Rachel Carson' (12).

Greater world attention was paid to the Greenpeace message in 1985 after the sinking of the *Rainbow Warrior.* The Greenpeace vessel was anchored in Auckland, New Zealand, and was preparing to bear witness to the French government's testing of nuclear bombs near Moruroa Atoll in the Pacific Ocean. Later, it was revealed that French secret agents were responsible for the boat's sinking and the drowning of one Greenpeace member on board. The tragedy brought unprecedented renown to Greenpeace. Since that time the organization has, among other things, worked to protect old growth forests, popularized the issue of climate change, and enlisted many more members worldwide than the handful that formed the original group in the late 1960s.

Citizen action was also an important ingredient in the post-war environmental thrust. As baby boomers began to assert themselves, their message within the realm of environmental politics became more all-encompassing. Pollution Probe, organized at the University of Toronto in 1969, first emerged as a professor-student action group focused on Great Lakes pollution. The university already had a reputation for its pioneering studies of aquatic ecology in Canada. Pollution Probe served as the genesis of contemporary environmental action as members mounted campaigns against the dumping of detergents and the widespread use of phosphates by household consumers, both of which had adverse effects on Great Lakes ecosystems.

What energized citizens, students, and faculty members most was the issue of detergent pollution in Ontario waters. With the baby boom and new immigration, the province's population swelled in the decades following the Second World War, growing from 3.7 million in 1941 to over 6 million in 1961. Economic advantage was also part of the province's good fortune, as heavy industries and services multiplied during this period. However, pollution of the water and air were often consequences of this growth. Soap and synthetic detergents were used to clean industrial gears as well as household laundry, and they were commonly discharged into open waters once spent. These non-biodegradable agents raise the water temperature in a process called eutrophication, which puts excessive nutrients into the water and can lead to a thick growth of plant life, which then chokes the oxygen supply and threatens aquatic life. Of more immediate concern, however, was the fact that townships in the vicinity of heavily industrialized Hamilton, Ontario, reported their drinking water polluted to the extent that it came from the tap with a foamy crest upon it. As early as 1962, the townships passed resolutions that called upon the province to ban the use and sale of synthetic detergents, which were suspected to be causing the problem. The province did not act immediately. In 1964, the matter of pollution in Lakes Ontario and Erie was referred to the IJC, the fourth time it had been asked to weigh in on such a matter since its inception in 1909. Living up to its moniker of 'environmental watchdog,' the IJC recommended that Canadian and American governments work with the provinces and states to purge phosphates from the municipal and industrial wastes that are destined for these lakes.

University students and professors joined the chorus of voices seeking an end to the fouling of the environment. In 1969, Pollution Probe emerged as a lightning rod of public action. One of the leading personalities of the World Wildlife Fund (Canada), Monte Hummel, was among the students who spearheaded the drive for a cleaner world. Pollution Probe staged a mock funeral for the polluted Don River, canvassed door-to-door, and took every opportunity to present its message citywide – even nationally – through the CBC and Toronto newspapers. It was to this group of energetic and dedicated young people that University of Toronto zoology professor Donald Chant referred when he urged, 'Let us heed the voice of youth' (Read 245). Members of Pollution Probe offered evidence before the IJC in the ongoing investigations concerning water quality, and urged an immediate ban on the sale and use of products that were causing the problem. They also targeted consumers in the hopes that change could be affected from the bottom up.

The citizen organization's actions aided in the passage of the Canada Water Act in 1970. Rapid change was realized: as of August 1970, only 20 per cent of phosphate content was allowed to be dumped into the lakes and tributaries, and that amount was to be reduced to a mere 5 per cent by the end of 1972. The legislative win was certainly important, but the true measure of Pollution Probe's success was that it brought the issue of pollution to the public consciousness in very direct ways, and backed up its demands for action by citing scientific research. In 1972, Canada and the United States entered into the Great Lakes Water Quality Agreement in which both sides pledged to restore and maintain the biological integrity of the Great Lakes Basin after decades of pollution.

On 22 April 1970, Canadians joined others around the world in celebrating Earth Day. However, due to the Canadian academic calendar (university students were finished school for the summer), the Canadian celebrations were low key and not well attended. As a result, groups such as Pollution Probe and the Canadian Council of Churches reorganized their collective energies and focused attention on 14 October 1970 as Survival Day, reasoning that more students (and presumably professors) would be able to participate mid-semester.

In the week prior to the celebration, Canada was alive with debate over the state of the environment. Letters to the editor and editorials appeared in the *Toronto Daily Star* addressing a wide spectrum of issues, such as second-hand smoke as a form of 'public air pollution,' the spectre of water diversion to the United States, and renewed interest in saving Quetico Provincial Park from logging. The group Zero Population Growth called to alleviate the stress caused by human reproduction, and a provincial minister drew attention to urban sprawl that he believed threatened the quality of rural life. The controversial writer Farley Mowat entered the fray and apocalyptically predicted in one article that only a disaster that halts technological progress and the expansion of cities could forestall future pollution. 'Damn few people will survive. But it's probably the only way the species can survive,' he warned ('Only disaster can halt pollution, writer claims' 2). Around the same time, there was a bicycle parade through the centre of the rain-soaked downtown that attracted two hundred cyclists, and which the Pollution Probe sponsors hoped would recruit others to abandon '"the costly cumbersome automobile" in favour of the non-polluting bike' ('It was a good day for ducks and cyclists' 1).

The most articulate expression of what was occurring in Toronto and elsewhere came from R.C. Elliott, a zoology professor at the University of Toronto. The occasion was the defence of a book that Pollution Probe had published, which addressed a plethora of environmental concerns. A reviewer had dismissed the book and branded ecologists as a 'cult of nature worshippers.' In response, Elliott made the argument that ecology was both a branch of the biological sciences as well as a label to describe the awareness of pollution and interest in its correction. 'Picture the earth as your garden,' Elliott urged. He used a metaphor that could easily be equated with human arrival in and departure from the Garden of Eden in order to help people understand his group's message. 'Ecologists maintain that the earth is a limited system,' Elliott continued, 'or, to use a very simple analogy: is like a garden of finite size. A small number of people can live well on the produce of that garden. As people increase, each individual must be content with less, if the produce is to be distributed evenly' (Elliott 7). In straightforward terms, he elaborated upon the system of energy flows and the necessity of preserving its soundness through the protection of all species. The *Toronto Daily Star* endorsed the idea of Survival Day, which used as its logo the Canadian flag with the maple leaf falling in mid-air. During that day's observance, public speeches were given by federal ministers in Ottawa on the state of the environment. In Toronto, Pollution Probe buried a time capsule at the corner of Harbord and St George streets and later held a debate on the sources of pollution at the University of Toronto's Convocation Hall.

From the mid-1970s to the end of the twentieth century, Canadians confronted a North American pollution problem: acid rain. Acid precipitation is as old as the earth itself. Carbon dioxide is a natural component of air that, when combined with rain, forms a trace solution of carbonic acid. Normally, such a naturally occurring process would yield a pH level of approximately 5.6; the neutral level is 7.0. Natural buffers such as limestone have regularly checked excessive elevations of the pH level. However, the industrial age introduced a variety of factors that altered such processes. This was especially true in the twentieth century as coal-generated power stations provided current to increasing numbers of manufactories. Nickel smelters, the refining of oil and gas, and the near-global use of the automobile became accepted features of the industrial and post-industrial age and also contributed to acid precipitation. In the past, incidents of pollution were local. But with the advent of greater production facilities and on larger scales, the problem became increasingly widespread. This situation was punctuated when smelters and coal-firing stations became equipped with very tall smokestacks. This allowed the chemical particles to mix more easily in the upper atmosphere and be more easily carried by air currents (the jet stream) in a west-to-east direction. This was the case first in Northern Europe, where British and German industrial plants deposited acid rain in Scandinavia during the 1950s and 1960s. The same phenomenon occurred in North America and was first recognized in Nova Scotia lakes in the mid-1950s; at that time it was presumed that the source of the pollutants was a great distance away to the west. Throughout the 1960s and 1970s a variety of manufactories emerged in the American Great Lakes states and in Ontario (most infamously at Sudbury, the largest nickel mining and

smelting site in the world, and around the so-called Golden
Horseshoe) that produced acid rain. (Even as early as the
1960s, lakes nearby Sudbury recorded loss of fish and it
was concluded that acid rain was the cause.) Acid rain,
snow, fog, and dry particles thus descended upon Canada
from Ontario to the Maritimes, and upon the United States
throughout the Northeast – especially New England. Acid
precipitation's effects are as varied as its sources. Aquatic
species are adversely affected as pH levels rise; the most
extreme cases result in lowered reproductive rates in fish.
Similarly, forests, soils, and crops deteriorate, threatening
ecosystems and those who rely most upon them for their
livelihoods: lumberers and farmers. In addition to such
social costs, recreationists from Ontario to the Maritimes
witnessed the decay of some of their most beloved landscapes, and anglers, especially at lakes in Northern Ontario
and Quebec, noticed that the waters had become crystal
clear, transparent to the extent that such sources ceased to
support aquatic life. They were 'acid dead.'

The Canadian Coalition on Acid Rain forcefully addressed
the issue. Founded in 1981, it became Canada's largest
environmental organization and made a name for itself as a
lobby group in both Canada and the United States. Michael
Perley and Adele Hurley were its executive coordinators
and prime lobbyists. For a good decade, the Coalition and
other smaller groups throughout Eastern Canada made
their voices heard. Ottawa and the provinces took steps to
curb Canadian pollutants in 1985. And the principal source
nation, the United States, finally moved to answer the calls
of Canadians and its own citizens. On 15 November 1990,
President George H.W. Bush signed the US Clean Air Act
into law. This became the basis for the 1991 Canada-US
Air Quality Agreement (with the IJC as oversight agency),
signed by Prime Minister Brian Mulroney and President
Bush in Ottawa on 13 March 1991. The agreement bound
both countries to reduce sulfur dioxide and nitrogen oxide
emissions and to cooperatively monitor air quality.

The State's Response

The federal state responded to the environmentalist impulse in several ways. First, it organized a 1961 federal-provincial conference, Resources for Tomorrow, that showcased research addressing many areas of common concern: forestry, wildlife, recreation, fisheries, and regional planning. The five-day conference dealt with issues germane to all regions, urban and rural. Dozens of panel sessions were held and eighty papers were heard. The rationale for the meeting was steeped in conservationist thinking (i.e., the discourse centred upon the conservation and management of resources). Indeed, in framing the historical context for such a gathering, the government drew upon longstanding touchstones of Canada's economic relationship with the rest of the world. F.J. Thorpe of the Department of Northern Affairs and National Resources wrote that 'the growing interest in resource development in Canada is attributable to many factors not the least of which is the need to meet increasing competition throughout the world. How well we meet this competition depends in no small measure on how well we manage our resources' (1). Consequently, the papers focused upon a set of ideas such as a countrywide assessment of resource supplies and greater coordination between the federal and provincial governments and companies involved in economic development in order to more systematically serve the needs of resource extraction and international trade. Yet, the conference organizers simultaneously recognized the rising concerns of environmental protection and the stress urban sprawl placed upon land, water, and air. Promoting access to clean recreational areas was also cited as a goal.

The period from the 1970s to the end of the twentieth century saw the advent of several pieces of federal legislation that seemed to answer the concerns that Canadians had voiced. In 1970, the Canada Water Act emerged in response to citizen action. In part due to contestation by the United States over Canada's sovereignty in the Arctic, the Arctic Waters Pollution Prevention Act of 1985 was passed. This legislation not only cemented Canada's claim over the region, but also sent the message that Canada did not approve of American nuclear submarines traversing the narrow Arctic passages. As well, Ottawa and the provinces agreed to stem Canadian emissions that contributed to acid precipitation (the Eastern Canada Acid Rain Program, 1985); this was done just prior to Canada entering into serious negotiations with the United States over the transboundary issue. On the world stage, Canadian Maurice Strong was co-chair of the United Nations Conference on the Human Environment (held in Stockholm in June 1972). The much-heralded gathering, described as 'pivotal . . . in the growth of the global environmental movement,' was the first instance in which such an international body had considered the desires and realities of economic growth alongside the health of the natural environment (McCormick 107).

Additional environmental policies and programs initiated by the federal government toward the end of the twentieth century served to protect Canadian waterways and animals. Responding to the public's desire for protection of and access to rivers, the federal, provincial, and territorial governments established the Canadian Heritage Rivers System (CHRS) in 1984. The goal was to promote wild rivers, mainly in the West and North, and to encourage citizen participation in celebrating their place in shaping the course of history. The genesis of the idea lay with Pierre E. Trudeau, the prime minister at the time and an avid canoeist. Today, the CHRS facilitates conservation programs that help to ensure the sustainability of the riverine environment for economic and recreational use. Furthermore, as Canadians sought better access to wild spaces, they also hoped to encounter and observe indigenous species. Such sentiments lay at the root of the 2003 Species at Risk Act, which protects species in danger of extinction and provides a starting point for their recovery.

At the start of the twenty-first century, Canada seems to be committed to two key agendas of environmental concern: the protection of resources and their continued exploitation. The former is exemplified by such protection measures as the Species at Risk Act, while the latter can be seen in industry – most notably the grand-scale oil sands project in Northern Alberta. Working to satisfy growing domestic and international demands, this megaproject mines rather than drills for oil at more than six facilities, which produce a combined three-quarters of a million barrels daily. Under Paul Martin's Liberal government, Canada signed the UN-led Kyoto Protocol (adopted in 1997 and ratified by the Canadian parliament in 2002). It bound Canada and thirty-six other industrialized countries, including the European community, to reduce greenhouse gas emissions between 2008 and 2012. Since then, however, Stephen Harper's Conservative government has not maintained the momentum needed to meet the targets set at Kyoto. Moreover, the high price of oil worldwide has made Alberta oil all the more attractive. Canada's place as both a producer and consumer of fossil fuels has put the country in a precarious position in the debate over global warming and climate change. As with the acid rain problem, Canada has also had to react cautiously to standards and policies pursued in Washington, DC, when setting its own greenhouse gas emission targets; it would be fruitless to be either under or over the American limits since the two nations share a continent. Indeed, it was precisely for this reason that Canada took a secondary position at the Copenhagen meeting on climate change in December 2009.

Conclusion

Concerted political action for the protection of the environment as a place of residence and a place of solace from

the frenetic urban world became a benchmark of 1960s
social awareness, along with other important issues such
as women's and Aboriginal rights. Older models of conservation and preservation faded as post-Second World War
demographic and social changes led to an eclipse of the
previous ways of seeing nature. The new message was more
global, thus yielding to the idea of human stewardship not
only for immediate resource issues (e.g., water quality in
the Great Lakes), but also for wider-ranging problems such
as acid rain and especially climate change. Yet there is a
paradox evident when considering our age of environmentalism. For all the protection of the environment during the
past fifty years, why is it that world environmental problems
such as water shortages, food crises, deforestation, and perhaps the most dangerous, global warming, are still with us?
The answer is complex and would certainly be well beyond
the scope of this brief text. On a basic level, however, it
might come down to the difference between assumptions
about what's possible and the limitations of reality. David
Suzuki encapsulated this very sentiment in a 1990 editorial.
Canadians, he wrote, assumed that local concerns like clean
drinking water, reduced litter through recycling, and generally healthier communities would translate into greater,
more omnibus plans for healing the planet. 'Think globally, act locally,' the belief that daily, incremental, personal
changes would yield a wholesale remedy on a global scale,
was the adage during the 1980s. But an economic recession
in Canada at the start of the 1990s shocked people out of
this frame of mind. How could economic security, premised
on the existence of inexpensive and plentiful supplies of
oil, coexist alongside a new and more ecologically sound
treatment of our natural world? In the post-Second World
War period, staples – especially petroleum and heavy minerals like ore and nickel – propelled the national economy
forward. Such confidence inspired and supported a range
of industrial projects and led to a commonplace assump-
tion that this foundation would be the economic bedrock
of the nation for generations to come. The current debate

over the Albert oil sands project is informed by the competing demands of environmental protection and resource
exploitation that I have addressed toward the end of this
chapter. Demand for oil, especially by the United States, is
high. The federal government seeks to balance economic
stability, regional growth, and reduced emissions, but this is
proving to be a tall order. The situation is complicated all
the more when one considers that the crude oil found in
the Alberta oil sands requires more refining than conven-
tional oil and thus even more fossil fuels must be burned
to convert it into a marketable commodity. Furthermore,
trees surrounding the oil sands must be cleared to make
way for the processing technology, which lessens the area
that could conceivably aid in absorbing carbon emissions
(a so-called carbon sink). Simultaneously, however, world
leaders speak of capping and trading emissions, whereby
limits are placed on each emitter; if they fall below that pre-
scribed mark, they can then trade their remaining credits
to polluters that exceed their own limits, with the effect of
limiting the total amount of pollutants emptied into the
atmosphere. The gap between what is desired and what is
possible appears wide. One can only hope that it will be
reduced as economic stability returns and governments,
in particular, move to more forcefully address the climate
change dilemma.

5

Aboriginal Canadians and Natural Resources: An Overview

An overview of recent environmentalism would be incomplete without considering the place of First Nations peoples in this historical movement. Chapter four, ostensibly, was about Canadians of non-Aboriginal descent and the government apparatus that they constructed. First Peoples have historically been excluded from the important decision making that shapes Canada's future; during the creation of the Canadian nation state, they were quite purposely pushed to the margins of society. The previous chapters have demonstrated just how intertwined with the natural environment our actions really are, and how the environment often influences the daily and long-term decisions we make. As well, because questions of natural resource use have different consequences for various actors in Canada's history (e.g., rural inhabitants or urban dwellers), elucidation is needed on how natural resource use affects Canada's First Peoples. This is all the more important in the contemporary period. Uses of forests and fisheries and concerns over air and water pollution have prompted new ways of framing policy for environmental protection. Aboriginal assertion over territory adds another dimension to this analysis and thus deserves greater scrutiny, as it gets at the heart of Aboriginal self-determination (both in a politico-cultural and economic sense).

As interest in the environment has been rekindled over the past half century, Aboriginal land claims and demands for greater autonomy over resources and the issues surrounding them have become closely linked to the contemporary environmental movement. Such claims have also sought to address longstanding social inequities and pave the way for Aboriginal self-governance (as the Inuit in Nunavut achieved). In other words, land and the natural resources it holds are central to the Aboriginal worldview, and have been for thousands of years. Recognizing that there can be competing discourses in contemporary Canada over the proper treatment of the natural environment provides an important starting point in the ongoing dialectic that is modern environmentalism. Aboriginal issues have become intertwined with environmental debates.

Indigenous Peoples in Recent History

How have Aboriginal issues come to influence the Canadian environmental movement? Part of the answer can be found in examining the world that emerged after the Second World War. The acceptance of the United Nations both in function and spirit assisted in prompting reflection on the consequences of European colonialism. In various regions of the world, cries for decolonization were heard. Indigenous peoples had long been protesting the loss of their lands and access to resources, and in the post-war era those in power finally seemed to appreciate this message. It seemed disingenuous for nations such as the United States, Canada, Australia, and New Zealand to criticize longstanding allies like Britain and France for being slow to recognize the self-determination of peoples in colonies such as Rhodesia (now Zimbabwe) or Indochina (Vietnam) when indigenous peoples within their own borders lived in second-class conditions and with little hope of bettering their socio-economic standing. Another important development was the 1948 adoption of the United Nations Universal Declarations of

Human Rights, which challenged liberal democracies to better provide for their poorest citizens. In Canada's case, this meant Aboriginal peoples.

Aboriginal issues have also come to influence the Canadian environmental movement through Native activism. Just prior to World War II, Aboriginal peoples in Canada more actively sought to challenge the status quo, and continued to do so for the next generation. Between 1923 and 1924, the Iroquois people took their claim of sovereignty to the League of Nations. Ultimately, however, British intervention caused the case to be dropped. In 1939, academics and policymakers invited Aboriginals to a conference on Native social issues cosponsored by Yale University and the University of Toronto. The meeting smacked of paternalism, with the conveners presenting ideas and a final report on what should be done to help the Natives. The Aboriginals in attendance responded with their own statement, declaring the need for an all-Native conference free from the interference of other North Americans.

A generation later, more prompts to action followed. In 1969, the Liberal government of Pierre E. Trudeau sought to alter the status of Aboriginals. In their White Paper, the Liberals proposed rapid assimilation by repealing the Indian Act of 1876, ending the reserve system, and abruptly cancelling an initiative by the previous Liberal government to enhance Aboriginal status. In an angry response, the Native Red Paper maintained that white-Aboriginal relations were and should be defined by treaties, but also called for special status. In 1969, the *Calder* case emerged as the first major land claims decision. Although the Nisga'a of northwestern British Columbia lost the case, it established a precedent whereby the federal government negotiated land claims based on outstanding Aboriginal titles. (By 2000, the Nisga'a did score a victory and a final agreement with the government, and what turned the case to their advantage was the Supreme Court of Canada's consideration of oral evidence in the proceedings.) Aboriginal and treaty rights received a degree of protection with the ratification of the Canadian Charter of Rights and Freedoms in 1982, and the birth of the Assembly of First Nations (which grew out of the National Indian Brotherhood) that same year spoke to the desire for a concerted Aboriginal political effort. That the patriation of the Canadian constitution gave a greater role to the Supreme Court in the process of determining policy is well known, and this also impacted Aboriginal land claims questions. In the late 1990s, for example, the *Marshall* decision (discussed below) and *Delgamuukw v. British Columbia* signalled a turning point in judicial advocacy and victories for First Peoples. In the latter court case, the idea of land title was broadened and clarified so that large expanses of land might be considered part of the claim, and oral and written evidence was given equal weight in determining a claim. Two years later, in 1999, the federal government established the territory of Nunavut, which meant de facto self-government by the Inuit majority.

Twentieth-century Aboriginal assertiveness at more elevated levels signalled not only a turning point among First Nations, but also in the way that Canadians viewed them. 'Celebrity Indians' such as Grey Owl (Archie Belaney, who was English born but pretended to be Native for most of his life) helped to create a mythic image of the 'ecological Indian,' which played upon the Enlightenment vision of Aboriginals as linked to the wilderness and as embodying the very essence of all things natural. Grey Owl's mystique and popularity during the 1930s came at a point when Aboriginals were squarely in the background of Canadian society. A masquerading Englishman reminding people that humans 'belong to Nature, and not it to you' (Loo 113) could easily pass off such sentiment as authentic Aboriginal spiritual belief. Grey Owl became an international star, so much so that the London *Times* heralded him as the 'Indian Thoreau' (after the nineteenth-century American naturalist Henry David Thoreau) (ibid.). As Tina Loo explains, '[f]or Grey Owl, conservation meant a return to simpler times, a return to the past. His was a nostalgic message, something that appealed in the tumultuous 1930s, an era of economic depression and looming war' (ibid. 116). Belaney's death in 1938 and the subsequent revelation of his elaborate hoax brought to an end the romanticized notion of the Aboriginal connection to nature. As well, serious scholarship revealed that First Peoples in the pre-encounter period shaped the land to best fit their needs by burning and clearing forest, hunting and fishing, horticulture and agriculture, and other such alterations that ensured their own survival. By no means should we perceive First Peoples as entirely benign in their treatment of the environment; recall the contemporaries who disparaged Aboriginal over-hunting during the fur trade era.

This is not to suggest, however, that First Peoples disregarded the health of animal populations or that they did not see the beaver's destruction as detrimental to their very own survival. An example from the twentieth century is illustrative of this very idea. During the 1930s, the HBC in northern Quebec conducted an experiment. It recognized that the global economic depression had forced down demand for furs. Yet, the company also recognized that a market still existed and that it was necessary to limit the number of beaver pelts taken so as to keep the price competitive. Rather than abandon the area, the HBC pursued a conservation policy that doubled as a social policy. The company was also aware of the well-being of its main supplier, the Cree. The beaver of the North, including around James Bay, were trapped out or had succumbed to disease; their numbers had been considerably thinned. With no pelts to trade or company credit to tide them over during the downturn, some Cree starved. The HBC drew upon past experience whereby they refused to take summer pelts and began organizing preserves, areas designated for the taking of furs. Moreover, the company put the Cree in charge of the sanctuary system, first at Rupert House, then at other spots in the area. Because their future livelihoods depended upon the success of the new regime, the Cree were diligent in maintaining the rules of capture and sale. The company also drew on the expertise of biologists who examined other aspects of the situation, such as the beaver's water and food sources. The program was a grand success and lasted into the 1950s, during which time the HBC was held up as a model for game management while the Cree proved to be efficient partners in the strategy. Similar preserves were established by the provincial governments of Manitoba and Saskatchewan and by private interests along the Saskatchewan River.

This brief example helps to illustrate the interplay and agency of Natives in our modern conception of conservation, as well as the paternalism of non-Aboriginals instructing Natives on how to manage their resources. However, the historical record prior to the mid-twentieth century was more often characterized by the limiting of Aboriginal access to natural resources, and the policy-making apparatus that regulated natural resource use.

Struggles for Resources

The era of conservation legislation brought about what Tina Loo refers to as the 'colonization' of rural spaces by urban elites (40). In other words, when sport hunting became actively promoted in the late nineteenth and early twentieth centuries, game laws were created to limit access to the staples of Aboriginal and rural Canadian diets. We have seen a similar scenario with the Atlantic salmon fishery. First Peoples came under special scrutiny when it came to the introduction of game and fish laws, for, according to the prevailing thought, removing the Natives from the wilderness and the perceived by-gone ways of hunting and gathering would hasten their move toward a sedentary, agricultural life and reinforce ideas of Western civilization. This was certainly the attitude among policymakers and legislators in industrializing Ontario at the turn of the twentieth century who defended the exclusion of First Peoples from the hunt. In 1906, a provincial Game and Fish Commission report bluntly stated that 'employment can now be procured in nearly all parts of the Province by those who want to work ... [Natives] should be made to either work or starve, and not be allowed to lead lazy loafing lives, destroying valuable assets of the Province with impunity' (Calverley 117). For these administrators, protecting game and fish for recreational hunting was more important than protecting those who relied upon hunting for food.

The advent of parks during the same period also signalled an exclusionary impulse. Rather than make space for First Peoples who inhabited places designated to be national or provincial parks, government bureaucrats moved them to the margins of parks land so as not to interfere with visitors' enjoyment. Recreationists at Banff National Park and Ontario's Point Pelee and Georgian Bay Islands National Parks did not welcome foraging Natives whom they believed would poach game and generally despoil the wilderness experience. At Banff, park administrators believed that a hunt by the Stoney band in the Canadian Rockies would thin the stock of animals. Administrators reckoned that a superabundance of wild, roaming animals was needed to attract visitors, so they banned the Stoneys' hunt. The result of such initiatives across the country was that traditional users were excluded from the very lands they claimed as their own, which they and their ancestors had accessed for centuries. When the automobile became a popular means of discovering Canadian national parks in the 1930s, officials at Manitoba's Riding Mountain similarly pushed a local band (the Keeseekoowenin Ojibwa) from the park's boundaries.

Colonization of Aboriginal space and resources occurred in subarctic regions as well. When caribou populations in the Northwest Territories diminished during the 1940s and 1950s, government scientists blamed Dene and Inuit hunting practices and physically resettled several families, in some cases to the High Arctic. Little effort was made to address the ancillary causes for caribou depletions, which included wolf predations, diseases, accidents, inclement weather (e.g., deep snow), and natural occurrences such as fire on the winter range. At work was an effort to stem human hunting, but also to push Aboriginal hunters into industrial wage labour wherever it existed in the North. Also, around Great Slave Lake, a generation of mining and industrial commercial fishing (often by non-Aboriginals) created public health hazards. Radiation poisoning and the discharge of fish offal into local water sources affected thousands. As both industries (which originated from outside of the region) waned in the early 1960s, some Aboriginal communities had to be relocated in the interest of protecting inhabitants. Thus colonization, displacement, and appropriation of resources were key themes of Aboriginal-white relations at least to the end of the twentieth century.

The path to modern environmentalism is replete with stories of dispossession and exclusion of Aboriginal peoples. To understand our twenty-first century situation, where First Nations peoples are reasserting their claims to land and resources, requires examining several key twentieth-century case studies to isolate and reveal a pattern. British Columbia's Clayoquot Sound forest, the Atlantic fishery, the natural gas frontier of the Mackenzie Valley in the Northwest Territories, and Quebec's James Bay hydroelectric project will be examined below.

Forest and Fishery

The 1990s controversy at Clayoquot Sound in British Columbia focused international attention on Canada in a remarkable way and altered the scenarios that had existed to that point. The situation on Vancouver Island's coast with its old-growth forests juxtaposed Aboriginals with environmentalists, and disrupted the latter's belief that the former unequivocally shared its vision of preservation. Lumbering

had long been important to the province's economy. However, by the 1990s, the clear-cutting of old growth timber at
Clayoquot Sound conflicted with the large tourist economy
sector, whose proponents worried that disappearing forests
would threaten their fortunes. Both mainstream and more
radical environmentalists (such as Greenpeace) joined
with Aboriginals to demonstrate. During the summer of
1993, a veritable 'war in the woods' ensued, although by
non-violent means. This included the Nuu-chah-nulth
First Nations' blockade of lumbering activities. All told,
approximately 9,000 people passed through the Clayoquot
Sound Peace camp that had been established by protestors;
ultimately, over 900 protestors were arrested on various
charges (750 for engaging in the blockade), making it the
largest display of civil disobedience in Canadian history
to date at the time. The seemingly common goal among
environmentalists and Aboriginals to defend resources
became complicated, however, as various bands in the area,
including the Nuu-chah-nulth, struck deals with the federal
and provincial governments. Such agreements gave Natives
some rights to log the lands themselves. Environmentalists
wanted a complete halt to the practice of logging, but First
Nations peoples wanted a more managed cull that would
allow them to set the pace and be compensated for the use
of the resource. In other words, Aboriginals wanted recognition that the land belonged to them. (In fact, the ultimate
realization of First Nations aspirations was a land-use plan
for the area that involved retention logging and benefited
Natives for this use.) By the end of 1993, Greenpeace found
it difficult to continue the blockade (in large part because
the New Democratic Party government had launched a law-
suit against protestors). The demonstration at Clayoquot
ended. The cleavages between these two groups, each with
their own particular methods, tactics, and goals for protecting the forest, had been revealed.

The story of the Atlantic coastal fisheries offers another
case of Aboriginal resource exclusion and restitution. In

1993, Donald Marshall, Jr., a Mi'kmaq with a long history of challenging the Canadian justice system (he had been wrongly accused of a murder and served prison time), was charged with catching eels without a licence. The case sparked a furore as Marshall challenged the Department of Fisheries and Oceans' (DFO) actions in court, arguing that his right to fish was protected by a longstanding treaty. Beginning in August 1993, Marshall was twice stopped by fisheries officials for contravening federal fisheries law, including taking eels in Pomquet Harbour, Cape Breton Island, without a licence and then attempting to sell the contraband catch. He challenged the government in court, arguing that he was only abiding by agreements between his people (the Mi'kmaq) and the British monarch signed in 1760 and 1761. The case served as a litmus test for the defence of treaty rights and was eventually heard before the Supreme Court of Canada in November 1998. In September 1999, the court handed down a majority ruling that Marshall was justified in taking fish, and, moreover, had the right to sell his catch. Non-Aboriginal fishers throughout the region worried that now even more competitors would enter the lucrative lobster fishery. DFO officers feared that Aboriginals would use the court's finding to ignore closed seasons and other conservation measures. At Burnt Church, on New Brunswick's north shore, controversy emerged not long after the Court's decision, when Aboriginals set a thousand lobster traps after the government-regulated season had closed. Non-Aboriginal fishers took direct action by confronting the Aboriginals on the water. In November 1999, however, the court clarified its initial decision. It stated that the ruling applied only to eels and not lobster or any other fish species or natural resources like timber. Importantly, the court also upheld the rights of non-Aboriginals to fish and make a living, and asserted that existing federal conservation policies prevailed over Aboriginals' right to fish; closed seasons, therefore, had to be obeyed. As in the case of Clayoquot Sound, a delicate balancing act was needed to diffuse heated situations between Aboriginal and non-Aboriginal Canadians when it came to the exploitation of natural resources.

The cases of recreationists in parks, the standoff at Clayoquot, and the tenseness and uncertainty in the Atlantic lobster fishery highlight instances in the claim of Aboriginals to their lands and resources. The exploitation of other resources, such as natural gas tapping and the harnessing of water current, extends the analysis of hinterland colonization in the complex and contested narrative of Aboriginals in Canada's environmental history.

Developing Resources

In the last section we considered case studies in which Aboriginal resources were objects of conservation, and often pitted Canadians with environmentalist agendas against First Peoples in a way that teased out the core differences between the two groups. Environmentalists assumed that Aboriginals were, or should be, 'ecological Indians.' When Aboriginals acted contrary to this ideal, wanting to exploit resources for their own sustenance or for profit, conservationists found themselves in an unexpected position, opposing the supposed 'original stewards of nature' and even sometimes summoning legal means to check what they saw as anti-conservationist Aboriginal behaviour. The debates in the previous section were concerned with protection of resources, while those in this section are about who gets to make decisions regarding the development of water current or extraction of fossil fuels and other minerals. The case of the Mackenzie Valley pipeline best exemplifies this debate.

In the 1970s, the pipeline debate centred upon the construction of a 4,200 km (2,625 mile) pipeline that would have carried natural gas from the shores of the Mackenzie Delta and Alaska's Prudhoe Bay south along the Mackenzie River Valley. From there, it could be connected to trans-shipment points in southern Canada and the United States. The federal government struck an inquiry commission chaired by Justice Thomas Berger, who sympathized with Aboriginal peoples and was a staunch defender of free speech. Justice Berger insisted that public hearings on the pipeline not only be conducted in Yellowknife, but in many other, much smaller venues throughout the region; in fact, the printed proceedings and testimony filled over two hundred volumes, enough to stock a small library. The parade of opponents who marched before the inquiry between 1974 and 1977 expressed concerns that environmental quality, a way of life, and local control of resources would be sacrificed for the pipeline project. Justice Berger came down on the side of the Aboriginals in his final report, recommending that no pipeline be built there for ten years, and thus allowing for outstanding land claims to be settled and greater diversification of the territorial economy to commence, lest the fortunes of stakeholders rise and fall with the whim of outside financial interests and capricious energy markets. Indeed, the case stands as a landmark in the contemporary debate over megaproject development and Aboriginal defence of their land.

The key Aboriginal actors along the proposed route (the Dene and Métis) were not so much anti-development in their thinking as they were determined to assert local control over decisions that would affect their surroundings and livelihoods. Concerns were raised not only over the environmental damage that the serpent-like pipeline could present to white whales in the delta and migrating caribou further south; more emphatically, the local Aboriginal people were concerned about the threats that such economic development might pose to their sociocultural milieu, where they were already seeing their children lose important connections to their heritage. Industrial endeavours such as oil extraction (after the 1920s discovery at Norman Wells, Northwest Territories), gold mining (spurred by the strikes around Great Slave Lake, the genesis of Yellowknife's boom period), and silver, copper, and lead-zinc mining had whetted the appetites of southern investors (Canadian and American) and hastened the industrialization of life in the North. Moreover, the millions of dollars invested in the region began to bring the southern Canadian lifestyle with its creature comforts to the North in ways that were not always appreciated by First Peoples. Some Dene elders worried that tested means of survival, such as the ability to make a fire while on hunting trips, were being lost with the passing of their generation. Fresh fish and moose meat, mainstays of the Dene and Métis diets, were being combined with processed foods bought in stores. Also, as post-Second World War fur prices declined, trapping became less desirable; Aboriginal subsistence increasingly depended upon a mixture of wage employment and government subsidies. Education in regional boarding schools further distanced northern Aboriginal children from their heritage, elders worried. Other (mainly younger) Dene community members worked to delay the pipeline project until the Dene themselves could gain more control over it. The Dene chief at Fort Good Hope, Frank T'Seleie (a man only in his twenties), punctuated hours upon hours of impassioned testimony when he addressed the Commission in August 1975, declaring 'My Nation will stop the pipeline' ('My Nation Will Stop the Pipeline'). Chief T'Seleie directed his history-laden attack specifically at Bob Blair, an oilman from Calgary, who also gave testimony, and whose company would have benefited from the pipeline:

You are like the Pentagon, Mr. Blair, planning the slaughter of the innocent Vietnamese . . . Don't tell me you are not responsible. You are the twentieth-century General Custer. You are coming with your troops to slaughter us and steal land that is rightfully ours. You are coming to destroy a people that have a history of thirty thousand years. Why? For twenty years of gas? Are you really that insane? ('In an Uncertain World')

Ultimately, in October 2001, the Dene and a consortium of gas and oil companies signed a memorandum of understanding, and in March 2011, a deal was struck to revive the pipeline. The Mackenzie Gas Project should deliver natural gas to more southerly points in North America, and may make the Dene shareholders of one-third of the profits.

Likewise, controversies surrounding the harnessing of rivers for hydroelectric power generation in Quebec led to a demand by Aboriginals to protect their resources and determine their uses. In the early 1970s, the Quebec government looked to its north, at James Bay, to further the generation of electricity. The project was immense: four dams in the province's north were designed to produce power for domestic US sale. The region's Cree people opposed the venture on the grounds that it would severely disturb their way of life that was closely tied to caribou, other fur-bearing animals, and fish. Premier Robert Bourassa announced the plan in April 1971. By autumn of that year, construction had begun on a road linking Matagami and the site of La Grande 2. Two years later, work began on the La Grande 2 site. The Cree sought a judicial injunction to halt the program, a motion that was initially granted, then overturned, prompting the Quebec government to submit an offer of settlement. By August 1974 the Aboriginals formed the Grand Council of the Cree to negotiate with the province. The moves led to the November 1975 signing of the James Bay and Northern Quebec Agreement that allowed the project to resume. More importantly, however, the move asserted a new self-determination as it established a 'tripartite land regime' by which the Cree and Inuit extinguished their title to the land, yet received other rights and benefits, including $275 million.

La Grande 2 became operational in late 1981. However, in September 1984, the worst fears of Aboriginals and environmentalists were confirmed when ten thousand deer were drowned after a spillway was opened on the Cania-piscau Reservoir. The Cree claimed that Hydro-Quebec had done this, a charge the utility denied. The drowning punc-

tuated the visible detriments to the resources and landscape. It followed, for example, decades of mercury release
that had poisoned fish, another Cree staple. The Aboriginal
stakeholders next turned to the international media in an
effort to draw attention their plight. In 1990, a group of
Cree led by their chief, Matthew Coon Come, paddled from
Ottawa to New York City, carrying the message that their
voices were left unheard while their natural environment
and way of life were suffering. The negative press heaped
upon the project and the apparent environmental spolia-
tion worked to undermine the lucrative contracts the Quebec government had drawn up with bordering American
states including Maine and New York, both of which with-
drew from agreements by the mid-1990s. New York State, in
particular, had reassessed its energy needs and decided that
the additional power was not needed. After this, the wider
scope of the project, including the proposed Great Whale
and the Nottaway-Broadback-Rupert phases of the overall
plan, drew outside attention, primarily of a critical nature.
Beleaguered, the province and the Cree made a new agreement in 2002 that gave the Cree $3.5 billion over fifty years,
plus more local control over their economy and the promise of more Hydro-Quebec jobs. Nearly 70 per cent of the
Cree favoured the agreement ('Cree and Québec').

These two case studies, it must be recalled, are informed
by centuries of white-Native relations during which time
Aboriginals have not prospered from European and Euro-
Canadian designs on the land, water, and their resources.
These case studies are also a by-product of the renaissance
of Native resistance that was brought about by the initiation
of the 1969 White Paper. Moreover, questions concerning
the use and future of resources directly touched the Dene
and the Cree, who had maintained their traditional ways
longer than many Aboriginal groups by virtue of where
they lived, in the Far North and Northern Quebec, where
contact with Euro-Canadians was sporadic and limited. In

the late twentieth century, technology and the demand for energy resources opened these parts of the continent to development debates in ways that had not occurred before.

Conclusion

The position of Aboriginal peoples in contemporary Canadian environmental debates raises questions of inclusion and exclusion. As we have seen in previous chapters, it is difficult to make the argument that the protection of the environment yields a value-free, win-win result for all affected parties. Recent global and national changes have given rise to increasingly vocal responses by First Nations peoples to environmental concerns that are often bound up in legal issues and land claims. For much of Canada's history, environmental questions have been addressed by Canadians of European descent. However, as the case of Clayoquot Sound revealed, assumptions by (usually white and urban) environmentalists that Aboriginals share their environmental agenda have failed to recognize the complexity of the Aboriginal position, which takes into account environmental sustainability and responsible stewardship of nature but also the livelihood of the local Aboriginal people. A similar scenario is playing out in northeastern Alberta, where environmentalists have decried the ruination of the landscape, the fouling of the Athabasca River and other water sources, the killing of aquatic life and birds, and the air pollution that are all side effects of the transformation of the oil sands into marketable oil for Canadian and American consumers. Yet, the Fort McKay First Nation has chosen to embrace the extraction of oil and form the Fort McKay Group of Companies, which services various aspects of the project. The Aboriginal-owned business reported a profit of $85 million in 2007, and the community now enjoys a low unemployment rate (of 5 per cent), a health clinic, a youth centre, and other perks. The community might even open a mine and produce oil on the more than eight thousand acres that it owns.

No longer can it be taken for granted that environmentalism means the same thing to all people. In regions of recent European settlement (such as Canada, the United States, Australia, and New Zealand) where contemporary citizens grapple with the legacy and meaning of the conquest of First Nations peoples, finding consensus for the notion of environmental stewardship can be difficult. The renaissance of Aboriginal assertiveness and the subsequent claims First Nations people have made over the land and its resources do not necessarily imply that the natural elements of the once-imagined 'Aboriginal way of life' will be treated in ways acceptable to (often white) urban/suburban middle- and upper-class recreationists. In the cases of Clayoquot Sound and Fort McKay, Aboriginals considered the extraction of their resources and the revenue that it could bring to be a means of protecting and sustaining their own communities. This attitude has complicated environmentalist agendas and forced a fundamental rethinking about the inclusiveness of their causes. After all, how can environmental policy be framed without taking the needs and desires of Aboriginal peoples into consideration as part of that larger debate?

Conclusion

What, then, is the road from here? Clearly, the interplay of humans and nature has been integral to the formation of Canada. The competing desires to exploit and protect natural resources serve as the central conflict in this dialectic. But that cannot be the end of this story. As we have seen, a vast array of other historical factors has influenced how we conceive of our place on earth and how we treat our natural surroundings. Indeed, that is part of the reason why a book like this is possible; as a species we have come to fully recognize that we belong to nature, and that in order to maintain not only our own, but other species' survival, we must be ever more cognizant of this fact. My interpretations throughout these chapters have landed on some rather pessimistic conclusions. Much of our present environmental dilemma, with issues such as global warming, rests on a perilous predicament: unless we somehow devise a means to replace our current dependence upon fossil fuels, we shall continue to emit gases into our atmosphere that contribute to climate change. Market forces dictate that Canada, as a leading oil producer (especially to a leading oil-consuming country, the United States), must exploit its resources to fill this demand on the world market. But as a result, Canada is contributing to what some forecast will be a global ecological catastrophe. As the historian J.R. McNeill has cogently stated, the planet's history and people's history remain tightly linked, perhaps more so now [in the twentieth century] than at most times past . . . [a]steroids and volcanoes, among other astronomical and geological forces, have probably produced more radical environmental changes than we have yet witnessed in our time. But humanity has not. This is the first time in human history that we have altered ecosystems with such intensity, on such scale and with such speed. (McNeill xxiv, 3)

Change has occurred quickly, and we have become the prime agents of it. Unless Canadians renounce involvement in the capitalist economic system, it seems unlikely that the situation will improve. This is hardly meant as a call to action, for most of us would only grudgingly give up the creature comforts that capitalism has brought. But if McNeill is correct, and we are the species responsible for the seemingly bleak future that awaits the earth, then real and substantial change on our part will have to happen soon. Although we share this planet with other living things, ultimately humans alone possess the intellect to overcome the environmental problems we have created. Recognizing our shared historical development alongside nature may well be the best spur to address the threats to our common future. It may be from this point of departure that future histories of Canada's environment will be written.

Selected Bibliography

Introduction

Cronon, William C. 'The Trouble with Wilderness, or Getting Back to the Wrong Nature.' *Environmental History* 1, no. 1 (January 1996): 7–28.

Chapter One

Ainley, Marianne Gosztonyi. 'Science in Canada's Backwoods: Catharine Parr Traill.' In Barbara T. Gates and Ann B. Shteir, eds., *Natural Eloquence: Women Reinscribe Science*, 79–97. Madison: University of Wisconsin Press, 1997.

Bavington, Dean. *Managed Annihilation: An Unnatural History of the Newfoundland Cod Collapse*. Vancouver and Toronto: University of British Columbia Press, 2010.

Berger, Carl. *Science, God, and Nature in Victorian Canada*. Toronto: University of Toronto Press, 1983.

Binnema, Theodore. *Common and Contested Ground: A Human and Environmental History of the Northwestern Plains*. Norman: University of Oklahoma Press, 2001.

Boivin, Bernard. 'Gaultier, Jean-François.' *Dictionary of Canadian Biography*. Vol. 3, *1741 to 1770*, 675–81. Toronto: University of Toronto Press, 1974.

Cadigan, Sean. *Newfoundland and Labrador: A History*. Toronto: University of Toronto Press, 2009.

Clark, Andrew Hill. *Acadia: The Geography of Early Nova Scotia to 1760*. Madison: University of Wisconsin Press, 1968.

Coates, Colin M. *The Metamorphoses of Landscape and Community in Early Québec*. Montreal and Kingston: McGill-Queen's University Press, 2000.

Colpitts, George. *Game in the Garden: A Human History of Wildlife in Western Canada to 1940*. Vancouver and Toronto: University of British Columbia Press, 2002.

Cook, Ramsay. 'Cabbages Not Kings: Towards an Ecological Interpretation of Early Canadian History.' *Journal of Canadian Studies* 25, no. 4 (Winter 1990–1): 5–16.

—. *Canada, Quebec, and the Uses of Nationalism*. 1986. Toronto: McClelland and Stewart, 1995.

Crosby, Alfred W. *The Columbian Exchange: Biological and Cultural Consequences of 1492*. Westport, CT: Greenwood Press, 1972.

—. *Ecological Imperialism: The Biological Expansion of Europe, 900–1900*. Cambridge: Cambridge University Press, 1986.

Darwin, Charles. *On the Origin of Species by Means of Natural Selection, or the Preservation of Favoured Races in the Struggle for Life*. London: John Murray, 1859.

—. *The Descent of Man, and Selection in Relation to Sex*. London: John Murray, 1871.

Delâge, Denys. *Bitter Feast: Amerindians and Europeans in Northeastern North America, 1600–64*. Trans. Jane Brierley. Vancouver and Toronto: University of British Columbia Press, 1993.

Dickason, Olive Patricia. *Canada's First Nations: A History of Founding Peoples from Earliest Times*. 3rd ed. Toronto: Oxford University Press, 2002.

—. *A Concise History of Canada's First Nations*. Toronto: Oxford University Press, 2006.

Dickenson, Victoria. 'Cartier, Champlain, and the Fruits of the New World: Botanical Exchange in the 16th and 17th Centuries.' *Scientia Canadensis* 31, no. 1 (2008): 27–47.

Dickinson, John, and Brian Young. *A Short History of Quebec*. 4th ed. Montreal and Kingston: McGill-Queen's University Press, 2008.

Duchesne, Raymond. 'Laflamme, Joseph-Clovis-Kemner.' *Dictionary of Canadian Biography Online*. Vol. 13, *1901–1910*. Web. Toronto: University of Toronto Press, 1994.

Dunlap, Thomas R. ' "The Old Kinship of Earth": Science, Man and Nature in the Animal Stories of Charles G.D. Roberts.' *Journal of Canadian Studies/Revue d'etudes canadiennes* 22, no. 1 (Spring 1987): 104–20.

—. 'The Realistic Animal Story: Ernest Thompson Seton, Charles G.D. Roberts, and Darwinism.' *Forest and Conservation History* 36, no. 2 (April 1992): 56–62.

Evans, Brian L. 'Ginseng: Root of Chinese-Canadian Relations.' *The Canadian Historical Review* 66, no.1 (March 1985): 1–26.

Evans, Clinton L. *The War on Weeds in the Prairie West: An Environmental History.* Calgary: University of Calgary Press, 2002.

Fiamengo, Janice. 'Looking at Animals, Encountering Mystery: The Wild Animal Stories of Ernest Thompson Seton and Charles G.D. Roberts.' *Journal of Canadian Studies/Revue d'etudes canadiennes* 44, no. 1 (Winter 2010): 36–59.

Forkey, Neil S. *Shaping the Upper Canadian Frontier: Environment, Society, and Culture in the Trent Valley.* Calgary: University of Calgary Press, 2003.

Gibson, James R. *Otter Skins, Boston Ships, and China Goods: The Maritime Fur Trade of the Northwest Coast, 1785–1841.* Montreal and Kingston: McGill-Queen's University Press, 1992.

Gosse, Philip Henry. *The Canadian Naturalist: A Series of Conversations on the Natural History of Lower Canada.* London: John Van Voorst, 1840.

Greer, Allan. *The People of New France.* Toronto: University of Toronto Press, 1997.

—, ed. *The Jesuits Relations: Natives and Missionaries in Seventeenth-Century North America.* Boston and New York: Bedford/St Martin's, 2000.

Griffiths, N.E.S. *From Migrant to Acadian: A North American Border People, 1604–1755.* Montreal and Kingston: McGill-Queen's University Press.

Hackett, Paul. *A Very Remarkable Sickness: Epidemics in the Petit-Nord, 1670 to 1846.* Winnipeg: University of Manitoba Press, 2002.

Hammond, Lorne. 'Marketing Wildlife: The Hudson's Bay Company and the Pacific Northwest, 1821–49.' *Forest and Conservation History* 37, no. 1 (January 1993): 14–25.

Harris, Cole. *The Resettlement of British Columbia: Essays on Colonialism and Geographical Change.* Vancouver: University of British Columbia Press, 1997.

—. *The Reluctant Land: Society, Space, and Environment in Canada Before Confederation.* Vancouver: University of British Columbia Press, 2008.

Harris, R. Cole, and John Warkentin. *Canada Before Confederation: A Study in Historical Geography.* Ottawa: Carleton University Press, 1995.

Hatvany, Matthew G. *Marshlands: Four Centuries of Environmental Change on the Shores of the St Lawrence.* Saite-Foy: Les Presses de l'Université Laval, 2003.

Heidenreich, Conrad E. 'Inland Expansion.' In R. Cole Harris, ed., *Historical Atlas of Canada,* Vol. 1: *From the Beginning to 1800,* plate 34, plate 35. Toronto: University of Toronto Press, 1987.

Hoeniger, J.F.M. 'Michaux, André.' *Dictionary of Canadian Biography.* Vol. 5, *1801 to 1820,* 592–3. Toronto: University of Toronto Press, 1983.

Innis, Harold A. *The Fur Trade in Canada.* New Haven: Yale University Press, 1930.

—. *The Cod Fisheries: The History of an International Economy.* New Haven: Yale University Press; Toronto: The Ryerson Press, 1940.

Jarrell, Richard A. 'Kalm, Pehr.' *Dictionary of Canadian Biography.* Vol. 4, *1771 to 1800,* 406–7. Toronto: University of Toronto Press, 1979.

Judd, Richard W. *The Untilled Garden: Natural History and the Spirit of Conservation in America, 1740–1840.* Cambridge and New York: Cambridge University Press, 2009.

Krech III, Shepard. *The Ecological Indian: Myth and History.* New York: W.W. Norton and Company, 1999.

Le Clercq, Chrestien. *New Relation of Gaspesia, with the Customs and Religion of the Gaspesian Indians.* Trans. and ed. William F. Ganong. Toronto: The Champlain Society, 1910.

Little, J.I. 'The Naturalist's Landscape: Philip Henry Gosse in the Eastern Townships, 1835–38.' *Journal of the Eastern Townships/Revue d'etudes des Cantons de l'Est* 20 (Spring 2002): 59–73.

Lower, A.R.M. *The North American Assault on the Canadian Forest: A History of the Lumber Trade Between Canada and the United States.* Toronto: The Ryerson Press; New Haven: Yale University Press, 1938.

Lutts, Ralph. *The Nature Fakers: Wildlife, Science, and Sentiment.* Golden, CO: Fulcrum, 1990.

MacNutt, W.S. 'The Politics of the Timber Trade in Colonial New Brunswick, 1825–1840.' In G.A. Rawlyk, ed. *Historical Essays on the Atlantic Provinces*, 122–40. Ottawa: Carleton University Press, 1967.

Morton, W.L. 'Victorian Canada.' In W.L. Morton, ed., *The Shield of Achilles: Aspects of Canada in the Victorian Age*, 311–34. Toronto: McClelland and Stewart, 1968.

Nelles, H.V. *The Politics of Development: Forests, Mines and Hydro-Electric Power in Ontario, 1849–1941.* Toronto: University of Toronto Press, 1974.

Owram, Doug. *Promise of Eden: The Canadian Expansionist Movement and the Idea of the West, 1856–1900.* Toronto: University of Toronto Press, 1980.

Perron, Jean-Marie. 'Provancher, Léon.' *Dictionary of Canadian Biography.* Vol. 12, *1891 to 1900*, 868–70. Toronto: University of Toronto Press, 1990.

Pyne, Stephen J. *Awful Splendour: A Fire History of Canada.* Vancouver and Toronto: University of British Columbia Press, 2007.

Roberts, Charles G.D. *The Kindred of the Wild: A Book of Animal Life.* Boston: Charles Livingston Bull Co., 1902.

Rousseau, Jacques. 'Sarrazin (Sarrasin), Michel.' *Dictionary of Canadian Biography.* Vol. 2, *1701 to 1740*, 593–600. Toronto: University of Toronto Press, 1969.

—. 'Brunet, Louis-Ovide.' *Dictionary of Canadian Biography.* Vol. 10, *1871 to 1880*, 105–7. Toronto: University of Toronto Press, 1972.

Saunders, R.M. 'The First Introduction of European Plants and Animals into Canada.' *The Canadian Historical Review* 16, no. 4 (December 1935): 388–406.

Seton, Ernest Thompson. *Wild Animals I Have Known.* New York: Charles Scribner's Sons, 1898.

Sheets-Pyenson, Susan. *John William Dawson: Faith, Hope, and Science*. Montreal and Kingston: McGill-Queen's University Press, 1996.

Traill, Catharine Parr. *The Backwoods of Canada: Being Letters from the Wife of an Emigrant Officer, Illustrative of the Domestic Economy of British America*. London: Nattali and Bond, 1836.

—. *Studies of Plant Life in Canada; Or, Gleanings from Forest, Lake, and Plain*. Ottawa: A.S. Woodburn, 1885.

Tyrwhitt-Drake, M.L. 'Douglas, David.' *Dictionary of Canadian Biography*. Vol. 6, *1821 to 1835*, 218–20. Toronto: University of Toronto Press, 1987.

Wadland, John Henry. *Ernest Thompson Seton: Man in Nature and the Progressive Era, 1880–1915*. New York: Arno, 1978.

Waiser, W.A. *The Field Naturalist: John Macoun, the Geological Survey, and Natural Science*. Toronto: University of Toronto Press, 1989.

White, Gilbert. *The Natural History of Selborne*. 1789. New York: Harper and Brothers, 1841.

Wood, J. David. *Making Ontario: Agricultural Colonization and Landscape Re-creation before the Railway*. Montreal and Kingston: McGill-Queen's University Press, 2000.

Worster, Donald. *Nature's Economy: A History of Ecological Ideas*. 1977. Cambridge and New York: Cambridge University Press, 1985.

Wynn, Graeme. *Timber Colony: A Historical Geography of Early Nineteenth Century New Brunswick*. Toronto: University of Toronto Press, 1981.

—. 'On the Margins of Empire (1760–1840).' In Craig Brown, ed., *The Illustrated History of Canada*, 189–278. Toronto: Lester and Orpen Dennys, 1987.

—. '"On Heroes, Hero-Worship, and the Heroic" in Environmental History.' *Environment and History* 10, no. 2 (May 2004): 133–51.

—. *Canada and Arctic North America: An Environmental History*. Santa Barbara: ABC-CLIO, 2007.

Zeller, Suzanne. *Inventing Canada: Early Victorian Science and Idea of a Transcontinental Nation*. Toronto: University of Toronto Press, 1987.

—. 'The Spirit of Bacon: Science and Self-Perception in the Hudson's Bay Company, 1830–1870.' *Scientia Canadensis* 13, no. 2 (Fall–Winter 1989): 79–101.

Chapter Two

Allardyce, Gilbert. ' "The Vexed Question of Sawdust": River Pollution in Nineteenth Century New Brunswick.' *Dalhousie Review* 52, no. 2 (Summer 1972): 177–90.

Armstrong, Christopher, Matthew Evenden, and H.V. Nelles. *The River Returns: An Environmental History of the Bow*. Montreal and Kingston: McGill-Queen's University Press, 2009.

Artibise, Alan F.J., and Gilbert A. Stetler. 'Conservation Planning and Urban Planning: The Canadian Commission of Conservation in Historical Perspective.' In Roger Kain, ed., *Planning for Conservation*, 17–36. New York: St Martin's Press, 1981.

Binnema, Theodore, and Melanie Niemi, ' "Let the line be drawn now": Wilderness, Conservation, and the Exclusion of Aboriginal People from Banff National Park in Canada.' *Environmental History* 11, no. 4 (October 2006): 724–50.

Bogue, Margaret Beattie. *Fishing the Great Lakes: An Environmental History, 1783–1933*. Madison: University of Wisconsin Press, 2000.

Bonnell, Jennifer. 'A Social History of a Changing Environment: The Don Valley, 1910–1931.' In Gene Desfor and Jennefer Laidley, eds., *Reshaping Toronto's Waterfront*, 123–50. Toronto: University of Toronto Press, 2011.

Bouchier, Nancy B., and Ken Cruikshank. ' "Sportsmen and Pothunter": Environment, Conservation, and Class in the Fishery of Hamilton Harbour, 1858–1914.' *Sport History Review* 28, no. 1 (May 1997): 1–18.

—. 'The War on the Squatters, 1920–1940: Hamilton's Boathouse Community and the Re-Creation of Recreation on Burlington Bay,' *Labour/Le Travail* 51 (Spring 2003): 1–32.

Canada, Commission of Conservation. *Report of the First Annual Meeting*. Ottawa: The Mortimer Co., Ltd., 1910.

Castonguay, Stéphane. *Protection des cultures, construction de la nature: Agriculture, foresterie et entomologie au Canada, 1884–1959.* Sillery, QC: Septentrion, 2004.

—. 'Foresterie scientifique et reforestation: l'Etat et la production d'une «foret a pate» dans la premiere moitie de xxe siècle.' *Revue d'Histoire de l'Amerique Francaise* 60, nos. 1–2 (Ete-Automne 2006): 61–93.

—. 'The Production of Flood as Natural Catastrophe: Extreme Events and the Construction of Vulnerability in the Drainage Basin of the St Francis River (Quebec), Mid-nineteenth to Mid-twentieth Century.' *Environmental History* 12, no. 4 (October 2007): 820–44.

—. 'Creating an Agricultural World Order: Regional Plant Protection Problems and International Phytopathology, 1878–1939.' *Agricultural History* 84, no. 1 (Winter 2010): 46–73.

Cox, Heather M., et al. 'Drowning Voices and Drowning Shoreline: A Riverside View of the Social and Ecological Impacts of St Lawrence Seaway and Power Project.' *Rural History* 10 (1999): 235–57.

Dagenais, Michèle. 'The Urbanization of Nature: Water Networks and Green Spaces in Montreal.' In Alan MacEachern and William J. Turkel, eds., *Method and Meaning in Canadian Environmental History*, 216–35. Toronto: Nelson, 2009.

Dagenais, Michèle, and Caroline Durand. 'Cleansing, Draining, and Sanitizing the City: Conceptions and Uses of Water in the Montreal Region.' *Canadian Historical Review* 87, no. 4 (December 2006): 621–51.

Dagenais, Michèle, and Stéphane Castonguay, eds., *Metropolitan Natures: Environmental Histories of Montreal.* Pittsburgh: University of Pittsburgh Press, 2011.

Dagenais, Michèle. *Montréal et l'eau. Une histoire environnementale.* Montréal: Les Éditions du Boréal, 2011.

Dorsey, Kurkpatrick. *The Dawn of Conservation Diplomacy: U.S.-Canadian Wildlife Protection Treaties in the Progressive Era.* Seattle: University of Washington Press, 1998.

Drushka, Ken. *Canada's Forests: A History.* Durham, NC: The Forest History Society; Montreal and Kingston: McGill-Queen's University Press, 2003.

Dyck, Jos. '"To Take the Food from Our Mouths": The Cow-ichans' Fight to Maintain Their Fishery, 1894–1914.' *Native Studies Review* 13, no. 1 (2000): 41–70.

Elliott, Henry W. *The Seal-islands of Alaska*. 1876. Kingston: Lime-stone Press, 1976.

Evans, Clinton L. *The War on Weeds in the Prairie West: An Environ-mental History*. Calgary: University of Calgary Press, 2002.

Evenden, Matthew D. 'The Laborers of Nature: Economic Orni-thology and the Role of Birds as Agents of Biological Pest Con-trol in North American Agriculture, ca. 1880–1930.' *Forest and Conservation History* 39, no. 4 (October 1995): 172–83.

—. *Fish versus Power: An Environmental History of the Fraser River*. Cambridge: Cambridge University Press, 2004.

—. 'La mobilisation des rivières et du fleuve pendant la Seconde Guerre mondiale: Québec et l'hydroélectricité, 1939–1945.' *Revue d'Histoire de l'Amerique Francaise* 60, nos. 1–2 (Ete-Automne 2006): 125–62.

—. 'Mobilizing Rivers: Hydro-Electricity, the State, and World War II in Canada.' *Annals of the Association of American Geogra-phers* 99, no. 5 (December 2009): 845–55.

Forkey, Neil S. 'Anglers, Fishers, and the St Croix River: Conflict in a Canadian-American Borderland, 1867–1900.' *Forest and Conservation History* 37, no. 4 (October 1993): 179–87.

—. 'Maintaining a Great Lakes Fishery: The State, Science, and the Case of Ontario's Bay of Quinte, 1870–1920.' *Ontario His-tory* 87, no. 1 (March 1995): 45–64.

—. *Shaping the Upper Canadian Frontier: Environment, Society, and Culture in the Trent Valley*. Calgary: University of Calgary Press, 2003.

Gillespie, Greg. *Hunting for Empire: Narratives of Sport in Rupert's Land, 1840–70*. Vancouver and Toronto: University of British Columbia Press, 2007.

Gillis, Robert Peter, and Thomas R. Roach. *Lost Initiatives: Can-ada's Forest Industries, Forest Policy and Forest Conservation*. New York: Greenwood Press, 1986.

Girard, Michel F. *L'écologie retrouvé. Essor et déclin de la Commission de la conservation du Canada*. Ottawa: Presses de l'Université d'Ottawa, 1994.

Grainger, M. Allerdale. *Woodsmen of the West*. 1908. Toronto: McClelland and Stewart, 1996.

Gulig, Anthony G. 'Sizing up the Catch: Native-Newcomer Resource Competition and the Early Years of Saskatchewan's Northern Commercial Fishery.' *Saskatchewan History* 47, no. 2 (Fall 1995): 3–11.

—. ' "Determined to burn off the entire country": Prospectors, Caribou, and the Denesuline in Northern Saskatchewan, 1900–1940.' *The American Indian Quarterly* 26, no. 3 (Summer 2002): 335–59.

—. ' "We Beg the Government": Native People and Game Regulation in Northern Saskatchewan, 1900–1940.' *Prairie Forum* 28, no. 1 (Spring 2003): 81–98.

Hak, Gordon. *Turning Trees into Dollars: The British Columbia Coastal Lumber Industry, 1858–1913*. Toronto: University of Toronto Press, 2000.

Harris, Douglas C. *Fish, Law, and Colonialism: The Legal Capture of Salmon in British Columbia*. Toronto: University of Toronto Press, 2001.

—. *Landing Native Fisheries: Indian Reserves and Fishing Rights in British Columbia, 1849–1925*. Vancouver: University of British Columbia Press, 2009.

Head, C. Grant. 'Economies in Transition.' In R. Louis Gentilcore, ed., *Historical Atlas of Canada*, Vol. 2, *The Land Transformed, 1800–1891*, 95. Toronto: University of Toronto Press, 1993.

—. 'The Forest Industry, 1850–1890,' plate 38. In R. Louis Gentilcore, ed., *Historical Atlas of Canada*, Vol. 2, *The Land Transformed, 1800–1891*. Toronto: University of Toronto Press, 1993.

Head, C. Grant, Rosemary E. Ommer, and Patricia A. Thornton. 'Canadian Fisheries, 1850–1890,' plate 37. In R. Louis Gentilcore, ed., *Historical Atlas of Canada*, Vol. 2, *The Land Transformed, 1800–1891*. Toronto: University of Toronto Press, 1993.

Hodgins, Bruce W., Jamie Benedickson, and Peter Gillis. 'The Ontario and Quebec Experiments with Forest Reserves, 1883–1930.' *Journal of Forest History* 26, no. 1 (January 1982): 20–33.

Howell, Colin D. *Blood, Sweat, and Cheers: Sport and the Making of Modern Canada*. Toronto: University of Toronto Press, 2001.

Hubbard, Jennifer. *A Science on the Scales: The Rise of Canadian Atlantic Fisheries Biology, 1898–1939.* Toronto: University of Toronto Press, 2006.

Ingram, Darcy. ' "Au temps et dans les quantités qui lui plaisent": Poachers, Outlaws, and Rural Banditry in Quebec.' *Histoire sociale/Social History* 42, no. 83 (Mai-May 2009): 1–34.

Jockel, Joseph T., and Alan M. Schwartz. 'The Changing Environmental Role of the Canada-United States International Joint Commission.' *Environmental Review* 8, no. 3 (Fall 1984): 236–51.

Jones, David C. *Empire of Dust: Settling and Abandoning the Prairie Dry Belt.* Edmonton: University of Alberta Press, 1984.

Keeling, Arn. 'Sink or Swim: Water, Pollution and Environmental Politics in Vancouver, 1889–1975.' *BC Studies* no. 142/143 (Summer/Autumn 2004): 69–101.

Knight, William. 'Samuel Wilmot, Fish Culture, and Recreational Fisheries in late 19th century Ontario.' *Scientia Canadensis* 30, no. 1 (2007): 75–90.

Kuhlberg, Mark. *One Hundred Rings and Counting: Forestry Education and Forestry in Toronto and Canada, 1907–2007.* Toronto: University of Toronto Press, 2009.

Langton, John. 'On the Age of Timber Trees, and the Prospects of a Continuous Supply of Timber in Canada.' *Transactions of the Literary and Historical Society of Quebec* 5 (1862): 61–79.

Leacy, F.H., ed. *Historical Statistics of Canada.* 2nd ed. Ottawa: Minister of Supply and Services Canada, 1983.

Little, J.I. 'Advancing the Liberal Order in British Columbia: The Role Played by Lieutenant-Governor Sir Hector-Gustave Joly de Lotbinière, 1900–1906.' *Journal of the Canadian Historical Association/Revue de la Société historique du Canada,* New Series, 19, no. 1 (2008): 83–113.

Little, James. *The Timber Supply Question, of the Dominion of Canada and the United States of America.* Montreal: Lovell Printing and Publishing Company, 1876.

Loo, Tina. *States of Nature: Conserving Canada's Wildlife in the Twentieth Century.* Vancouver: University of British Columbia Press, 2006.

Marsh, George Perkins. *Man and Nature; Or, Physical Geography as Modified by Human Action.* 1864. Ed. David Lowenthal. 1864. Cambridge: The Belknap Press of Harvard University Press, 1965.

Manore, Jean L. *Cross-Currents: Hydroelectricity and the Engineering of Northern Ontario.* Waterloo: Wilfrid Laurier University Press, 1999.

Massell, David. *Amassing Power: J.B. Duke and the Saguenay River, 1897–1927.* Montreal and Kingston: McGill-Queen's University Press; Durham, NC: Forest History Society Inc., 2000.

McInnis, Marvin. 'Elements of Population Change,' plate 28. In Donald Kerr, ed., *Historical Atlas of Canada,* Vol. 3, *Addressing the Twentieth Century, 1891–1961.* Toronto: University of Toronto Press, 1990.

Measner, Don, and Christine Hampson. 'The Canadian Population, 1871, 1891,' plate 29. In R. Louis Gentilcore, ed., *Historical Atlas of Canada,* Vol. 2, *The Land Transformed, 1800–1891.* Toronto: University of Toronto Press, 1993.

Murton, James. *Creating a Modern Countryside: Liberalism and Land Resettlement in British Columbia.* Vancouver and Toronto: University of British Columbia Press, 2007.

Nelles, H.V. *The Politics of Development: Forests, Mines and Hydro-Electric Power in Ontario, 1849–1941.* Toronto: University of Toronto Press, 1974.

Newell, Diane. *Tangled Webs of History: Indians and the Law in Canada's Pacific Coast Fisheries.* Toronto: University of Toronto Press, 1993.

Parenteau, Bill. ' "Care, Control and Supervision": Native People in the Canadian Atlantic Salmon Fishery, 1867–1900." *The Canadian Historical Review* 79, no. 1 (March 1998): 1–35.

—. 'A "Very Determined Opposition to the Law": Conservation, Angling Leases, and Social Conflict in the Canadian Atlantic Salmon Fishery, 1867–1914.' *Environmental History* 9, no. 3 (July 2004): 436–63.

Parenteau, Bill, and James Kenny. 'Survival, Resistance, and the Canadian State: The Transformation of New Brunswick's Native Economy, 1867–1930.'*Journal of the Canadian Historical Association/Revue de la Société historique du Canada,* New Series, 13, no. 1 (2002): 49–71.

Parr, Joy. *Sensing Changes: Technologies, Environments, and the Everyday,* 1953–2003. Vancouver and Toronto: University of British Columbia Press, 2009.

Piper, Liza. 'Parasites from "Alien Shores": The Decline of Canada's Freshwater Fishing Industry.' *The Canadian Historical Review* 91, no. 1 (March 2010): 87–114.

Pyne, Stephen J. *Awful Splendour: A Fire History of Canada.* Vancouver and Toronto: University of British Columbia Press, 2007.

Rajala, Richard J. *Clearcutting the Pacific Rain Forest: Production, Science, and Regulation.* Vancouver: University of British Columbia Press, 1998.

Rodgers, Andrew Denny. *Bernhard Eduard Fernow: A Story of North American Forestry.* Durham, NC: Duke University Press, 1991.

Sandlos, John. 'Federal Spaces, Local Conflicts: National Parks and the Exclusionary Politics of the Conservation Movement in Ontario, 1900–1935.' *Journal of the Canadian Historical Association/Revue de la Société historique du Canada,* New Series, 16, no. 1 (2005): 293–318.

—. *Hunters at the Margins: Native People and Wildlife Conservation in the Northwest Territories.* Vancouver and Toronto: University of British Columbia Press, 2007.

Sifton, Clifford. 'Address of Welcome to the City Planning Conference (1914).' In Paul Rutherford, ed., *Saving the Canadian City: The First Phase, 1880–1920,* 213–19. Toronto: University of Toronto Press, 1974.

Stunden Bower, Shannon. *Wet Prairie: People, Land, and Water in Agricultural Manitoba.* Vancouver and Toronto: University of British Columbia Press, 2011.

Thoms, J. Michael. 'A Place Called Pennask: Fly-fishing and Colonialism at a British Columbian Lake.' *BC Studies* 133 (Spring 2002): 69–98.

Tough, Frank. *'As Their Natural Resources Fail': Native Peoples and the Economic History of Northern Manitoba, 1870–1930.* Vancouver: University of British Columbia Press, 1996.

Van West, John J. 'Ojibwa Fisheries, Commercial Fisheries Development and Fisheries Administration, 1873–1915: An Examination of Conflicting Interest and the Collapse of the Sturgeon

Fisheries of the Lake of the Woods.' *Native Studies Review* 6, no. 1 (1990): 31–65.

Walton, Izaak, and Charles Cotton. *The Compleat Angler.* 1653. Edited by John Buxton with an introduction by John Buchan. Oxford: Oxford University Press, 2008.

Wirth, John D. *Smelter Smoke in North America: The Politics of Transborder Pollution.* Lawrence: University Press of Kansas, 2000.

Zeller, Suzanne. 'Darwin Meets the Engineers: Scientizing the Forest at McGill University, 1890–1910.' *Environmental History* 6, no. 3 (July 2001): 428–50.

Chapter Three

Altmeyer, George. 'Three Ideas of Nature in Canada, 1893–1914.' *Journal of Canadian Studies/Revue d'etudes canadiennes* 11, no. 3 (August 1976): 21–36.

Armstrong, Christopher, Matthew Evenden, and H.V. Nelles. *The River Returns: An Environmental History of the Bow.* Montreal and Kingston: McGill-Queen's University Press, 2009.

Bentley, D.M.R. 'Charles G.D. Roberts and William Wilfred Campbell as Canadian Tour Guides.' *Journal of Canadian Studies/Revue d'etudes canadiennes* 32, no. 2 (Summer 1997): 79–99.

Berger, Carl. 'The True North Strong and Free.' In Peter Russell, ed., *Nationalism in Canada,* 3–26. Toronto: McGraw-Hill, 1966.

Bordo, Jonathan. 'Jack Pine – Wilderness Sublime or the Erasure of the Aboriginal Presence from the Landscape.' *Journal of Canadian Studies/Revue d'etudes canadiennes* 27, no. 4 (Winter 1992–93): 98–128.

Brown, Robert Craig. 'The Doctrine of Usefulness: Natural Resources and National Park Policy in Canada, 1887–1914.' In J.G. Nelson and R.C. Scace, eds. *Canadian National Parks: Today and Tomorrow,* Vol. 1, 46–62. Calgary: University of Calgary, 1968.

Campbell, Claire Elizabeth. *Shaped by the West Wind: Nature and History in Georgian Bay.* Vancouver: University of British Columbia Press, 2005.

—, ed. *A Century of Parks Canada, 1911–2011*. Calgary: University of Calgary Press, 2011.

Coates, Colin M. *The Metamorphoses of Landscape and Community in Early Québec*. Montreal and Kingston: McGill-Queen's University Press, 2000.

Cook, Ramsay. 'Landscape Painting and National Sentiment in Canada.' *Historical Reflections* 1, no. 1 (June 1974): 263–83.

Cronin, J. Keri. *Manufacturing National Park Nature: Photography, Ecology, and the Wilderness Industry of Jasper*. Vancouver and Toronto: University of British Columbia Press, 2011.

Crowley, John E. ' "Taken on the Spot": The Visual Appropriation of New France for the Global British Landscape.' *The Canadian Historical Review* 86, no. 1 (March 2005): 1–28.

Dewar, Helen. 'Old World Conventions, New World Curiosities: North American Landscapes Through European Eyes.' *Journal of the Canadian Historical Association/Revue de la Société historique du Canada*, New Series, 14, no. 1 (2003): 45–63.

Dobak, William. 'Killing the Canadian Buffalo, 1821–1881.' *Western Historical Quarterly* 27, no. 1 (Spring 1996): 33–52.

Dunlap, Thomas R. 'Ecology, Nature, and Canadian National Park Policy: Wolves, Elk, and Bison as a Case Study.' In Rowland Lorimer et al., eds., *To See Ourselves/To Save Ourselves: Ecology and Culture in Canada* [*Conscience et survie: écologie et culture au canada*], 139–49. Montreal: Association for Canadian Studies/ Association d'etudes canadiennes, 1991.

Foster, Janet. *Working for Wildlife: The Beginning of Preservation in Canada*. Toronto: University of Toronto Press, 1978.

Grant, George Monro. *Picturesque Canada: the Country as It Was and Is*. 2 vols. Toronto: Belden Brothers, 1882.

Harding, Brian, and Ellen Harding. 'Looking Forward; Looking Backward: American and Canadian Scenery in the 1830s.' *British Journal of Canadian Studies* 8, no. 2 (September 1993): 163–79.

Hart, E.J. (Ted). *J.B. Harkin: Father of Canada's National Parks*. Edmonton: University of Alberta Press, 2010.

Hébert, Yves. 'Conservation, culture et identité: La creation du Parc des Laurentides et du Parc de la Montagne Tremblante,

1894–1938.' In John S. Marsh and Bruce Hodgins, eds., *Changing Parks: The History, Future and Cultural Context of Parks and Heritage Landscapes*, 140–59. Toronto: Natural Heritage, 1998.

Hémon, Louis. *Maria Chapdelaine*. 1914. Illus. Gilles Tibo. Trans. Alan Brown. Introd. Roch Carrier. Montréal: Tundra, 1989.

Jasen, Patricia. *Wild Things: Nature, Culture, and Tourism in Ontario, 1790–1914*. Toronto: University of Toronto Press, 1995.

Jessup, Lynda. 'The Group of Seven and the Tourist Landscape in Western Canada, or The More Things Change . . .' *Journal of Canadian Studies/Revue d'etudes canadiennes* 37, no. 1 (Spring 2002): 144–79.

—. 'Landscapes of Sport, Landscapes of Exclusion: The "Sportsman's Paradise" in Late-Nineteenth-Century Canadian Painting.' *Journal of Canadian Studies/Revue d'etudes canadiennes* 40, no. 1 (Winter 2006): 71–123.

Jones, Karen R. *Wolf Mountains: A History of Wolves Along the Great Divide*. Calgary: University of Calgary Press, 2002.

Kaufmann, Eric. ' "Naturalizing the Nation": The Rise of Naturalistic Nationalism in the United States and Canada.' *Comparative Studies in Society and History* 40, no. 4 (October 1998): 666–95.

Kheraj, Sean. 'Improving Nature: Remaking Stanley Park's Forest, 1888–1931.' *BC Studies* 158 (Summer 2008): 63–90.

Killan, Gerald. 'Mowat and a Park Policy for Niagara Falls, 1873–1887.' *Ontario History* 70, no. 2 (June 1978): 115–35.

—. *Protected Places: A History of Ontario's Provincial Parks System*. Toronto: Dundurn Press, 1993.

Little, J.I. 'Canadian Pastoral: Promotional Images of British Colonization in Lower Canada's Eastern Townships During the 1830s.' *Journal of Historical Geography* 29, no. 2 (April 2003): 189–211.

—. 'Scenic Tourism on the Northeastern Borderland: Lake Memphremagog's Steamboat Excursions and Resort Hotels, 1850–1900.' *Journal of Historical Geography* 35, no. 4 (October 2009): 716–42.

MacEachern, Alan. "Rationality and Rationalization in Canadian National Parks Predator Policy." In Chad Gaffield and Pam Gaffield, eds., *Consuming Canada: Readings in Environmental History*, 197–212. Toronto: Copp-Clark, 1995.

—. *Natural Selections: National Parks in Atlantic Canada*, 1935–1970. Kingston and Montreal: McGill-Queen's University Press, 2001.

MacLaren, I.S., ed. *Culturing Wilderness in Jasper National Park: Studies in Two Centuries of Human History in the Upper Athabasca River Watershed*. Edmonton: University of Alberta Press, 2007.

Moray, Gerta. *Unsettling Encounters: First Nations Imagery in the Art of Emily Carr*. Vancouver and Toronto: University of British Columbia Press, 2006.

Murton, James. 'La « Normandie du Nouveau Monde »: la société Canada Steamship Lines, l'antimodernisme et la promotion du Québec ancien.' *Revue d'histoire de l'Amérique française* 55, no. 2 (Été 2001): 3–44.

Osborne, Brian S. "The Iconography of Nationhood in Canadian Art." In Denis Cosgrove and Stephen Daniels, eds., *The Iconography of Landscape: Essays on the Symbolic Representation, Design and Use of Past Environments*, 162–78. Cambridge and New York: Cambridge University Press, 1988.

Pollock-Ellwand, Nancy. 'Rickson Outhet: Bringing the Olmsted Legacy to Canada: A Romantic View of Nature in the Metropolis and the Hinterland.' *Journal of Canadian Studies/Revue d'etudes canadiennes* 44, no. 1 (Winter 2010): 137–83.

Reichwein, Pearlann. '"Hands Off Our National Parks": The Alpine Club of Canada and Hydro-development Controversies in the Canadian Rockies, 1922–1930.' *Journal of the Canadian Historical Association/Revue de la Société historique du Canada*, New Series, 6, no. 1 (1995): 129–55.

Savard, Félix-Antoine. *Master of the River*. Trans. Richard Howard. Montreal: Harvest House, 1976.

Taylor, C.J. 'Legislating Nature: The National Parks Act of 1930.' In Rowland Lorimer et al., eds., *To See Ourselves/To save Ourselves: Ecology and Culture in Canada* [*Conscience et survie: écologie et culture au Canada*], 125–37. Montreal: Association for Canadian Studies/Association d'études canadiennes, 1991.

Thorner, Thomas, ed. '*A Country Nourished on Self-Doubt': Documents in Post-Confederation Canadian History*. 2nd ed., 238–50. Peterborough: Broadview, 2003.

Trofimenkoff, Susan Mann. *The Dream of Nation: A Social and Intellectual History of Québec.* Toronto: Gage, 1983.

Wall, Karen, and Pearlann Reichwein. 'Climbing the Pinnacle of Art: Learning Vacations at the Banff School of Fine Arts, 1933–1959.' *The Canadian Historical Review* 92, no. 1 (March 2011): 69–105.

Wall, Sharon. *The Nurture of Nature: Childhood, Antimodernism, and Ontario Summer Camps, 1920–55.* Vancouver and Toronto: University of British Columbia Press, 2009.

Chapter Four

Anastakis, Dimitry. 'A "War on Pollution"? Canadian Responses to the Automotive Emissions Problem, 1970–80.' *The Canadian Historical Review* 90, no. 1 (March 2009): 99–136.

Atwood, Margaret. *Surfacing.* 1972. New York: Anchor Books, 1998.

Back, Frédéric. 'agir ensemble/caring together.' Web. 18 July 2010. <http://www.fredericback.com>.

Bocking, Stephen. *Ecologists and Environmental Politics: A History of Contemporary Ecology.* New Haven: Yale University Press, 1997.

Bodsworth, Fred. *Last of the Curlews.* 1954. Toronto: McClelland and Stewart, 1991.

'Bush to sign act to reduce acid rain.' *Edmonton Journal* 15 (Nov. 1990): A14.

Canada. Statistics Canada. *Historical Statistics of Canada.* Section A: Population and Migration. Table A1: Estimated Population of Canada, 1867 to 1977. Web. 19 July 2010.

Carson, Rachel. *Silent Spring.* Boston: Houghton Mifflin, 1962.

Chant, Donald A., ed. *Pollution Probe.* Toronto and Chicago: New Press, 1970.

Davenport, Paul. 'Economics.' *The Canadian Encyclopedia,* n.d. Web. 4 June 2009.

Elliott, R.C. 'Picture the earth as your garden.' *Toronto Daily Star.* 12 October 1970: 7.

Forkey, Neil S. '"Thinking like a River": The Making of Hugh MacLennan's Environmental Consciousness.' *Journal of Canadian Studies/Revue d'etudes canadiennes* 41, no. 2 (Spring 2007): 42–64.

Freedman, Bill, et al. 'Species at Risk in Canada.' In Karen Beazley and Robert Boardman, eds., *Politics of the Wild: Canada and Endangered Species*, 26–48. Don Mills, ON: Oxford University Press, 2001.

Godbout, Jacques. *Dragon Island.* 1976. Trans. David Ellis. Don Mills: Musson, 1978.

Harris, Richard. *Creeping Conformity: How Canada Became Suburban, 1900–1960.* Toronto: University of Toronto Press, 2004.

Hays, Samuel P. *Beauty, Health, and Permanence: Environmental Politics in the United States, 1955–1985.* Cambridge and New York: Cambridge University Press, 1987.

Henripin, Jacques. 'Baby Boom.' *The Canadian Encyclopedia*, n.d. Web. 4 June 2009.

Howard, Ross, and Michael Perley. *Acid Rain: The Devastating Impact on North America.* New York and Toronto: McGraw-Hill, 1980.

'It was a good day for ducks and cyclists.' *Toronto Daily Star.* 13 October 1970, Metro ed.: 1.

Jones, Karen R. *Wolf Mountains: A History of Wolves Along the Great Divide.* Calgary: University of Calgary Press, 2002.

—. '*Never Cry Wolf*: Science, Sentiment, and the Literary Rehabilitation of *Canis Lupus.*' *The Canadian Historical Review* 84, no. 1 (March 2003): 65–93.

Keeling, Arn, and Robert McDonald. 'The Profligate Province: Roderick Haig-Brown and the Modernizing of British Columbia.' *Journal of Canadian Studies/Revue d'etudes canadiennes* 36, no. 3 (Fall 2001): 7–23.

Keeling, Arn. '"A Dynamic, Not a Static Conception": The Conservation Thought of Roderick Haig-Brown.' *Pacific Historical Review* 71, no. 2 (May 2002): 239–68.

Kenny, James L., and Andrew G. Secord. 'Engineering Modernity: Hydroelectric Development in New Brunswick, 1945–1970.' *Acadiensis* 39, no. 1 (Winter/Spring 2010): 3–26.

Kunzig, Robert. 'Scraping Bottom.' *National Geographic* (March 2009). Web. 9 September 2009. <http://ngm.nationalgeograph ic.com/2009/03/canadian-oil-sands/kunzig-text>.

Leacy, F.H., ed. *Historical Statistics of Canada.* 2nd ed. Ottawa: Minister of Supply and Services Canada, 1983.

Lightfoot, Gordon. 'The Wreck of the Edmund Fitzgerald.' *Summertime Dream.* Reprise, 1976. CD.

Lutts, Ralph H. 'The Trouble with Bambi: Walt Disney's *Bambi* and the American Vision of Nature.' *Forest and Conservation History* 36, no. 4 (October 1992): 160–71.

MacDonald, L. Ian. 'Canada should be comfortable with the Copenhagen pact.' *The Gazette* (Montréal) 13 December 2009. Web 29 June 2010.

MacLennan, Hugh. *Seven Rivers of Canada.* Toronto: Macmillan of Canada, 1961.

—. *Rivers of Canada.* Toronto: Macmillan of Canada, 1974.

McLaughlin, Mark J. 'Green Shoots: Aerial Insecticide Spraying and the Growth of Environmental Consciousness in New Brunswsick, 1952–1973.' *Acadiensis* 40, no. 1 (Winter/Spring 2011): 3–23.

McCormick, John. *The Global Environmental Movement.* 2nd ed. New York: John Wiley and Sons, 1995.

Mitchell, Jeannine. '"Cherry Point vs Life," February 10–17, 1971.' In Thomas Thorner, ed., *A Country Nourished on Self-Doubt: Documents in Canadian History, 1867–1980,* 454–8. Peterborough: Broadview Press, 1998.

Mitchell, Joni. 'Big Yellow Taxi.' *Ladies of the Canyon.* Reprise. 1970. CD.

Mowat, Farley. *Never Cry Wolf.* Boston: Little, Brown Co., 1963.

—. *A Whale for the Killing.* Boston: Little, Brown Co., 1972.

—. *Sea of Slaughter.* Toronto: McClelland and Stewart, 1984.

'Only disaster can halt pollution, writer claims.' *Toronto Daily Star.* 14 October 1970: 2.

Read, Jennifer. '"Let us heed the voice of youth": Laundry Detergents, Phosphates and the Emergence of the Environmental Movement in Ontario.' *Journal of the Canadian Historical Association/Revue de la Société historique du Canada,* New Series 7, no. 1 (1996): 227–50.

Robinson, Danielle. 'Modernism at a Crossroad: The Spadina Expressway Controversy in Toronto, Ontario, ca. 1960–1971.' *The Canadian Historical Review* 92, no. 2 (June 2011): 295–322.

Suzuki, David. 'Responsibility for the environmental crisis begins at home.' *The Gazette* (Montréal) 7 April 1990: A2.

Thorpe, F.J. 'Historical Perspective on the "Resources for Tomorrow" Conference,' in *Resources for Tomorrow*, Vol. 1: *Conference Background Papers*, 1–13. Ottawa: Queen's Printer, 1961.

United Nations. United Nations Framework Convention on Climate Change. 'Kyoto Protocol.' Web. 21 July 2010. <http://unfccc.int/kyoto_protocol/items/2830.php>.

Warecki, George M. *Protecting Ontario's Wilderness: A History of Changing Ideas and Preservation Politics, 1927–1973*. New York: Peter Lang, 2000.

Weyler, Rex. *Greenpeace: How a Group of Journalists, Ecologists, and Visionaries Changed the World*. Vancouver: Raincoast Books, 2004.

Zelko, Frank. 'Making Greenpeace: The Development of Direct Action Environmentalism in British Columbia.' *BC Studies* nos. 142/143 (Summer/Autumn 2004): 197–239.

Chapter Five

Binnema, Theodore and Melanie Niemi, ' "Let the line be drawn now": Wilderness, Conservation, and the Exclusion of Aboriginal People from Banff National Park in Canada.' *Environmental History* 11, no. 4 (October 2006): 724–50.

Calverley, David. ' "When the Need for It No Longer Existed": Declining Wildlife and Native Hunting Rights in Ontario, 1791–1898.' In Jean L. Manore and Dale G. Miner, eds., *The Culture of Hunting in Canada*, 105–20. Vancouver and Toronto: University of British Columbia Press, 2007.

—. 'The Dispossession of the Northern Ojibwa and Cree: The Case of the Chapleau Game Preserve.' *Ontario History* 101, no. 1 (Spring 2009): 83–103.

Carlson, Hans M. *Home is the Hunter: The James Bay Cree and Their Land*. Vancouver and Toronto: University of British Columbia Press, 2008.

Coates, Kenneth. *A Global History of Indigenous Peoples: Struggle and Survival.* New York: Palgrave Macmillan, 2004.

'Cree and Quebec Sign Landmark Deal.' *The National.* Canadian Broadcasting Corporation. 7 Feb. 2002. *CBC Digital Archives.* Web. 11 August 2009.

Dickason, Olive Patricia. *A Concise History of Canada's First Nations.* Toronto: Oxford, 2006.

Francis, Daniel. *The Imaginary Indian: The Image of the Indian in Canadian Culture.* Vancouver: Arsenal Pulp Press, 1992.

Francis, R. Douglas, Richard Jones, Donald B. Smith. *Destinies: Canadian History Since Confederation.* 6th ed. Scarborough: Nelson, 2008.

'In an Uncertain World.' *Canada: A People's History.* Canadian Broadcasting Corporation. 14 Nov. 2001. Television. 11 August 2009.

Keeling, Arn, and John Sandlos. 'Environmental Justice Goes Underground? Historical Notes from Canada's Northern Mining Frontier.' *Environmental Justice* 2, no. 3 (2009): 117–25.

Krech, Shepard, III. *The Ecological Indian: Myth and History.* New York: W.W. Norton and Company, 1999.

Kunzig, Robert. 'Scraping Bottom.' *National Geographic* March 2009. Web.

Loo, Tina. *States of Nature: Conserving Canada's Wildlife in the Twentieth Century.* Vancouver and Toronto: University of British Columbia Press, 2006.

Mackenzie Gas Project. Web. 11 August 2009. <http://www.mac kenziegasproject.com>.

'Mackenzie pipeline OK'd by cabinet, energy board.' *CBC News.* Canadian Broadcasting Corporation. 10 Mar. 2011. Web. 14 March 2011.

'Matthew Coon Come paddles to New York.' *As It Happens.* Canadian Broadcasting Corporation. 27 Mar. 1990. *CBC Digital Archives.* Web. 11 August 2009.

'My Nation Will Stop the Pipeline.' *CBC Television News.* Canadian Broadcasting Corporation. 5 Aug. 1979. *CBC Digital Archives.* Web. 11 August 2009.

Piper, Liza. *The Industrial Transformation of Subarctic Canada*. Vancouver and Toronto: University of British Columbia Press, 2009.

Ray, J. Arthur. *The Canadian Fur Trade in the Industrial Age*. Toronto: University of Toronto Press, 1990.

Sabin, Paul. 'Voices from the Hydrocarbon Frontier: Canada's Mackenzie Valley Pipeline Inquiry, 1974–1977.' *Environmental History Review* 19, no. 1 (Spring 1995): 17–48.

Sandlos, John. 'Federal Spaces, Local Conflicts: National Parks and the Exclusionary Politics of the Conservation Movement in Ontario, 1900–1935.' *Journal of the Canadian Historical Association/Revue de la Société historique du Canada*, New Series, 16, no. 1 (2005): 293–318.

—. *Hunters at the Margins: Native People and Wildlife Conservation in the Northwest Territories*. Vancouver and Toronto: University of British Columbia Press, 2007.

—. 'Not Wanted in the Boundary: The Expulsion of the Keeseekoowenin Ojibway Band from Riding Mountain National Park.' *The Canadian Historical Review* 89, no. 2 (June 2008): 189–221.

Turkel, William J. *The Archive of Place: Unearthing the Pasts of the Chilcotin Plateau*. Vancouver and Toronto: University of British Columbia Press, 2007.

Warner, Stanley. 'The Cree People of James Bay: Assessing the Social Impact of Hydroelectric Dams and Reservoirs.' In James F. Hornig, ed., *Social and Environmental Impacts of the James Bay Hydroelectric Project*, 93–120. Montreal and Kingston: McGill-Queen's University Press, 1999.

Wilson, Jeremy. *Talk and Log: Wilderness Politics in British Columbia, 1965–96*. Vancouver: University of British Columbia Press, 1998.

Wright, Miriam. ' "Building the Great Lucrative Fishing Industry": Aboriginal Gillnet Fishers and Protests over Salmon Fishery Regulations for the Nass and Skeena Rivers, 1950s–1960s.' *Labour/Le Travail* 61 (Spring 2008): 99–130.

—. 'Aboriginal Gillnet Fishers, Science, and the State: Salmon Fisheries Management on the Nass and Skeena Rivers, British Columbia, 1951–1961.' *Journal of Canadian Studies/Revue d'etudes canadiennes* 44, no. 1 (Winter 2010): 5–35.

Young, Oran. 'Introduction to the Issues.' In James F. Hornig, ed., *Social and Environmental Impacts of the James Bay Hydroelectric Project*, 3–18. Montreal and Kingston: McGill-Queen's University Press, 1999.

Conclusion

McNeill, J.R. *Something New Under the Sun: An Environmental History of the Twentieth-Century World.* New York: W.W. Norton and Company, 2000.

Index

Themes in Canadian History

Editors:
Colin Coates 2003–
Craig Heron 1997–
Franca Iacovetta 1997–1999

PROPERTY OF
SENECA COLLEGE
LIBRARIES
NEWNHAM CAMPUS